Suicide

Other Books in the *Pastoral Responses* Series

Addiction by Bucky Dann

Sexual Abuse by Len Hedges-Goettl

Suicide

PASTORAL RESPONSES

Loren L. Townsend

EDITED BY DANIEL G. BAGBY

ABINGDON PRESS

NASHVILLE

SUICIDE
PASTORAL RESPONSES

Copyright © 2006 by Abingdon Press

This book is printed on acid-free paper.

Library of Congress Cataloging-in-Publication Data

Townsend, Loren L.
  Suicide: pastoral responses / Loren L. Townsend ; edited by Daniel G. Bagby.
     p. cm.
  ISBN 0-687-49297-1 (pbk. : alk. paper)
  1. Suicide—Moral and ethical aspects. 2. Suicide—Religious aspects—Christianity. 3. Church work with the bereaved. 4. Pastoral counseling. I. Bagby, Daniel G. II. Title.

HV6545.T69 2006
259'.428—dc22

                                                          2005035240

All scripture quotations unless noted otherwise are taken from the *New Revised Standard Version of the Bible,* copyright 1989, by the Division of Christian Education of the National Council of the Churches of Christ in the United States of America. Used by permission. All rights reserved.

Scripture quotations marked KJV are from the King James or Authorized Version of the Bible.

06 07 08 09 10 11 12 13 14 15—10 9 8 7 6 5 4 3 2 1
MANUFACTURED IN THE UNITED STATES OF AMERICA

Contents

114937

Foreword

No one likes to talk about suicide. In some families, it remains the "family secret." Church families often have little notion of how to respond to church members who have experienced the loss of a loved one by suicide. In the aftermath of a completed attempt on one's own life, those left behind struggle to cope with bewilderment, grief, helplessness, and faith. Stunned family members and friends of the deceased often turn to the local church for answers and comfort, whether they are members of a congregation or not. We are never fully prepared for death, but the unexpected self-inflicted death is especially difficult. Where do we turn for understanding and nurture after such a tragedy? Loren Townsend has helped us all with some clear, gentle, practical assistance on the matter of suicide. He begins by giving his reader a concise picture of the incidence of suicide in the human family, its dynamic and occurrence by gender and age, and its known preexisting conditions and characteristics.

Readers will find biblical and historical background that explains some of the church's different interpretations to the act of suicide over the centuries.

Townsend, a therapist and minister himself, next identifies specific signs in depression that point toward lethality and the need for intervention where possible and describes issues a caregiver or minister may explore in the face of significant depression or a suicide attempt. He is helpful to ministers in the local church, by reflecting on the boundaries and limitations that clergy possess in responding to such difficult crises. He also assists the church and its leadership in finding ways to assist the bereaved congruent with their own gifts and limitations as the family of God. Medical, psychological, and spiritual resources and family care are offered in these pages, and pastor, layperson, and congregation will find them immensely useful in responding to this often silent and always tragic crisis.

Daniel G. Bagby, Ph.D.
Theodore F. Adams Professor of Pastoral Care
Baptist Theological Seminary at Richmond

Introduction

When Kathy Armistead at Abingdon Press asked me to write a needed book on suicide, I was not enthusiastic. Such a project would be time-consuming and emotionally draining. Suicide is not a cheery subject. Certainly, a number of my clients in nearly thirty years of clinical practice have been suicide survivors. Many more were depressed and considering suicide. Over the years I've responded to suicides in schools, churches, and businesses as a therapist trained in crisis and trauma debriefing. I also teach suicide assessment and response to developing pastoral counselors. Nevertheless, I felt reluctant to write this book and yet strangely drawn to it against my own and my wife's best judgment. Only as I came to the last stages of writing did I understand more clearly why my ambivalent "no" resulted in "yes."

In the fall of my third grade in school, my father's business partner took his own life. His wife came home from work and found him in the dining room. He had discharged a shotgun through the roof of his mouth. A note next to his body asked his wife for forgiveness and explained that his cancer had returned. He could not face more treatment. Adults gathered and whispered. Grisly images formed in my eight-year-old mind. I did not need the help of 1980s and 1990s Hollywood special effects to imagine what a 12-gauge shotgun would do to human flesh. I had seen what my father's gun did to birds and effortlessly transferred those memories to our family's close friend. No one spoke outright about his suicide or what it meant. No one knew what to do with an eight-year-old's nightmares or first real acquaintance with violent death. That school year my family moved from one coast to another. And then moved again. And then again. My father never spoke of his personal loss or how he was affected by his best friend's death.

When I was a sixth grader in Seattle, a teacher in my elementary school died suddenly without explanation. No adult spoke of her death except to say that she was gone. Nevertheless, her suicide was an open secret. When I was in junior high school, the mother of a neighborhood friend took her life with an overdose of pills. It was the 1960s. My mother took pills too. She was upset much of the time. Would she be next? My friend moved. No one talked about her mother's suicide. After my high school years, a close friend lost her father to suicide. He retired, became depressed, and shot himself. His wife found him in the backyard. Our families were active members of the same church. Suicide was a hushed, barely audible murmur within the congregation. As far as I know, there was no pastoral response. His surviving wife was a good friend of my mother. Mrs. "J" remained depressed and in psychiatric care until she died a decade later from health complications.

As these memories returned, I understood why I could not say "no" to this project. I don't think my experience is particularly unique. More than thirty thousand Americans die each year from suicide. Most people and most congregations must confront suicide at some point. Suicide is personal. It is theological. It is congregational. It becomes a permanent part of individual and congregational narratives. It is important that pastors have resources to respond when suicide comes home.

PURPOSE

This book assumes that pastors are frequent "first responders" to suicide; pastors are often the first called to support a family in a suicide emergency. Suicidal thoughts are often expressed first to pastors or other religious leaders who have caring, listening relationships with parishioners. Pastors are frequently called to care for individuals or family members after a spouse, parent, or child has unsuccessfully attempted suicide. In the wake of suicide's many forms, pastors may feel drawn into a web of life and death for which they were not trained. My first goal for this book is to provide a frame for understanding suicide, suicidal thinking, and suicide attempts. These are common human events that, if misunderstood, can increase suicide risk in a congregation. A second goal is to propose a set of strategies for congregational care along the continuum of suicidal behavior. The third goal is to propose liberative praxis as a method that can help guide the process of care and theological reflection on suicide.

Suicide is steeped in emotional experience—often depression—that challenges the foundation of life. It is expressed through a range of thought and action that extends from fleeting thoughts of self-harm to completing one's own death. Chapter 1 provides a brief introduction to suicide as a personal, historic, and religious phenomenon. The remainder of the book will follow the continuum of suicide through assessment of and response to suicidal thoughts, care when an attempt has been unsuccessful, and response when a suicide has been completed. Chapter 3 explores research in religion and mental health and offers an analysis of congregational practices and suicide risk. This book does not address ethical issues of assisted suicide and is not intended to articulate a developed theology of suicide. Instead, rather than answering theological questions about suicide, this book suggests a theological method that leads pastors and congregations toward new questions and revised answers that make sense in specific social locations. In the course of human history, suicide has posed questions that seem to defy answers. At the same time, surviving or preventing suicide means deeply engaging those questions of existence and meaning that are inevitably raised when someone takes his or her own life.

FOUNDATIONS: SUICIDE IN SOCIAL AND RELIGIOUS CONTEXT

Suicide is not new. Anthropological studies show that it has been with us since the dawn of human existence. The ability to think about meaning—a human distinction—seems to live hand in hand with the capability to end one's life intentionally and with forethought. This observation led Camus to conclude that "there is only one truly serious philosophical question, and that is suicide."[1] Suicide is part of our earliest collective social, cultural, and religious memory. Art, myth, and religious symbols in nearly every culture include images of and construct meanings for self-killing. From earliest human history, suicide and religion are inescapably joined.

Roots in Antiquity

Anthropological evidence shows self-killing has always been a part of human experience. It appears to be a fundamental part of collective human self-consciousness.[2] As human society increased in complexity, so did the role and meaning of taking one's life. The history of Western culture shows that suicide has had a variety of meanings across time and culture.

In Greek and Roman stories, self-killing was a resolute act of voluntary death. It was an act of will using rope, swords, or daggers that rarely left room for failure. Images of ancient suicides remain in our language and symbols today. Ajax, for instance, is a name portraying resolute strength. Historically, Ajax was a soldier recognized as a hero of the Trojan War second only to Achilles. However, following Achilles's death, he lost the debate with Ulysses to inherit Achilles's armor. Unable to live with this blow to his honor, Ajax fell on his own sword and ended his life. He was immortalized as a model of honor and resolution. Greek soldiers for generations wore a bronze likeness of Ajax as part of their battle armor. Another example, Lucrece, a female hero symbol, took her own life to retain honor and underscore her claim that she was raped by a Roman prince. Like Ajax, her figure appears frequently in Roman art and literature and endures as a common name.

Ancient literature frequently celebrates noble people who voluntarily ended their lives in service to excellence or in response to potential shame. Roman literature alone records more than a thousand suicides of philosophers, politicians, and warriors. Self-killing was also an accepted form of execution (illustrated by Nero's order that Stoic philosopher Seneca end his own life) and a way to resolve forbidden love. The Roman playwright Ovid (43 BCE–18 CE) cast the figures of Pyramus and Thisbe in roles that framed suicide as the highest symbol of romantic devotion sixteen hundred years before Romeo and Juliet. Even so, these glorified meanings of suicide were not universally accepted. Plato, whose thought was influential in both Greek and Roman history, was opposed to any form of suicide. In his book of *Laws*, Plato asserted that those who take their own life frustrate the decree of destiny. This is an act of abject cowardice unless it is forced by a state decree, loss of mental abilities because of calamity, or a desperate and intolerable disgrace. Suicide is a violation that requires victims to be buried "ignominiously in waste and nameless spots"[3] without marker or headstone. These teachings became the ground of Augustine's theology of suicide in the fourth century CE.

Judeo-Christian Tradition

Suicide, though rare, is part of our heritage in the Judeo-Christian tradition. Though biblical Hebrew has no word for suicide, there are five clear cases of self-inflicted death in the Hebrew Bible. The first recorded suicide is found in Judges 9:53. Abimelech, ruler of the Northern Kingdom, was wounded seriously in battle by a millstone thrown by a female defender. Rather than bear the disgrace of being killed by a woman, he instructs his armor bearer to kill him. Scripture makes it clear that his death was punishment for his unrighteous action. In Judges 16, Samson is humiliated and tormented by the Philistines. He prays for strength and pulls the roof down upon himself and the Philistines. His death is interpreted historically as both a suicide and a heroic act to liberate his people. King Saul's death (1 Sam. 31) is a third example of suicide. Wounded in battle and facing certain humiliation by the Philistines, Saul takes his own life.* Second Samuel 16–17 records the story of Ahitophel, who joined Absalom's rebellion against David. He later lost his position with Absalom and hanged himself. Zimri (1 Kings 16) is the final example of Old Testament suicide. Seven days after he assassinated King Elah in an attempted coup, Zimri is surrounded by the opposition. Rather than surrender or be killed, he burns the citadel and ends his own life in the fire.

These stories share a common factor. Each death was stimulated by extreme humiliation or a military defeat that would have led either to shame or disgraceful death. In one case (Samson), suicide seems to be an act of heroism after a shameful series of decisions. Ahitophel and Zimri were both condemned because of rebellion—life cut short by their own hand was the consequence of their sin. Apart from these observations, issues of suicide morality do not arise in the biblical text. There is no concern for the *postmortem* welfare of the victim, no sense of punishment for taking one's own life or denial of burial.

Rabbinic tradition takes a much stronger stand on suicide. God alone grants life. Taking any life, including one's own, is prohibited except in very specific circumstances. Tormented souls, Moses (Num. 11), Elijah (1 Kings 19), Job (Job 6), and

---

*This account is complicated by two accounts of Saul's death. In 1 Samuel 31, Saul is forced to take his own life when his armor bearer refuses to kill him. In 2 Samuel 1, David punishes an Amalekite soldier who reported that he killed the badly wounded Saul.

Jonah (Jon. 4) may cry for God to end suffering through death, but killing one's self is not an individual right. Willful suicide is strictly prohibited in the Midrash and Mishneh Torah, the law code of Maimonides. One who willingly commits suicide is to be denied burial and may be denied life in the hereafter. However, a judgment of "willful suicide" demands very strict proof. The Babylonian Talmud (Semahot 2:2) sets criteria. First, fatal action must be declared before witnesses (plural), prepared before witnesses, and immediately carried out in the presence of witnesses. Later authorities required even more substantial proof. No death that follows hours or days after a declaration or that takes place without witnesses can be declared a suicide. When circumstances suggest a suicide, willful suicide cannot be assumed. The Shuchan Aruch (sixteenth century) excluded minors from willful suicide and adults (specifically King Saul) when they were trapped in impossible circumstances.[4]

It is clear that, except for extreme cases, taking one's life is seen as an irrational act for which a person is not morally responsible. Even the word for suicide in Rabbinic Hebrew, *abed et atzmo*, literally translated means "loses himself."[5] Jewish law allows that a death may not be judged a "willful suicide," even in the face of legal or medical evidence that one has taken his or her own life. This tradition is rooted in deep pastoral concern for survivors. Even in rare cases of "willful suicide," mourning rites and honorable burials needed by the family were not withheld.

Suicide is also part of our Gospel heritage. It is clear that Judas killed himself after betraying Jesus. Like Old Testament stories, New Testament writers condemned Judas for betraying Jesus, but say nothing about his suicide. Early Christian attitudes toward suicide are hard to evaluate. Some scholars suggest that Christianity's ambivalence about suicide rests in the central images of crucifixion. Scripture affirms that Jesus chose the way of the cross. He willingly walked into a situation that he knew would kill him. No matter what the expected outcome, this image provides a symbol of heroic choice of self-death on behalf of others. Likewise, Paul's attitude that "to die is gain" (Phil. 1:21 KJV) and his choice to go to an almost certain death in Rome can be interpreted as self-destruction guided by the Holy Spirit.[6] Exploring the hermeneutical and theological meanings of such claims is beyond the scope of this text. However, they do illustrate a ground for Christian ambivalence about life, death, and suicide acted out in martyrs who threw themselves onto funeral pyres, who embraced the Roman soldiers who would kill them, or who drowned themselves rather than be defiled. Deep within our Christian heritage lie basic questions of the value of physical, earthly life. When is it better to die than to live? Under what circumstances is self-determined death part of the story of redemption or, conversely, a betrayal of God's gift of life?

Early Christian documents reveal tension when veneration of martyrs encouraged suicidal behavior. This is illustrated in a difference of opinion between Ignatius of Antioch (d. 107 CE) and Polycarp (c. 70–155 CE), both of whom were killed for their faith. On one hand, Ignatius actively pursued a unity with Christ that he believed could be realized only in a martyr's death. He sought to become the "food of wild beasts" and "God's wheat to be ground into Christ's pure bread."[7] Polycarp, on the other hand, firmly stated that he would not commend those who presented themselves for martyrdom. This was "not the teaching of the gospel."[8] In either case, those who died because of persecution (actively pursued or not) became enduring symbols of commitment and faith.

In the fourth century, suicide was formally opposed by church doctrine as a pastoral concern. Responding to an incident of group suicide by women anticipating rape, Augustine declared that, while Scripture did not prohibit suicide, neither did it make it lawful. To stop martyr suicides, he declared that the commandment against killing applied also to killing one's self. As if to highlight historic Christian ambivalence, Augustine (*City of God*, Book I, Sections

18–26) left room for suicide that might be "ordered by God." This doctrine was later affirmed at the Council of Braga (563 CE). Thomas Aquinas expanded the church's interpretation with a less ambiguous statement that established suicide as the one sin that could not be forgiven. One could not confess murder after death. These two doctrines have guided most Christian thinking about suicide. They are reflected in Catholic and Orthodox theology, both of which have historically embraced martyrs and barred those who have taken their own life from burial in consecrated cemeteries. The view of suicide as inherently sinful is also reflected in Protestant statements such as the Westminster Shorter Catechism (1647), which states that the sixth commandment forbids suicide, and Dietrich Bonhoeffer's *Ethics,* which asserts that suicide undermines God's will. Current Protestant thought on suicide tends to affirm that life is a gift of God and that God will not give a person more suffering than can be endured. To take one's life is a failure of faith because it sets limits on how much suffering we think we can endure.[9]

Contemporary theological analysis of suicide retains a fundamental ambivalence. Messages of unforgivable sin and breaking the sixth commandment are still present within conservative Catholic, mainline Protestant, and evangelical traditions. However, progressive Catholic, mainline Protestants, and evangelical theologians have moved away from categorically condemning suicide. This is observed in the debate about assisted suicide and denominational statements that focus on suicide as a pastoral concern rather than a theological doctrine. One example is the United Methodist document, "Suicide: A Challenge to Ministry."[10] This document recognizes the ways in which contemporary statements about suicide have oppressed both victims and survivors. Concern is focused on recognizing societal factors that create conditions for suicide and expressing pastoral concern for those who are alienated and at risk for suicide. This statement affirms that it is not the church's task to judge, but to participate actively as an advocate for those who are at risk and to minister to survivors.

MINISTRY IN AN AMERICAN CULTURE

Our American context reflects deep ambivalence about suicide inherited from multiple influences. In-depth social analysis of suicide in the United States is beyond the purpose of this book. However, pastors in the United States must attend to complex images and attitudes that form the context of suicide in this particular social location. There is no "American" attitude toward suicide. Our cultural approach to taking one's life is an ethnic, religious, and political mosaic. In some cases we hold up images of heroes who sacrificed their own lives to respond to the tragedy of 9/11, who stood firm in their patriotism at the expense of their own lives, or who chose certain death to achieve important goals. In other cases, we condemn Jonestown and the Branch Davidians. We thrill to cinema that portrays a brave "everyman" who crashes his spaceship into a comet to save Earth (*Deep Impact*) and the distressed father who is willing to allow police to shoot him or to shoot himself to get medical care for his son (*John Q*). We argue both the pros and the cons of assisted suicide for those for whom life no longer holds hope.

If we listen carefully, we can hear some social analysts suggest that Americans are fundamentally suicidal. We live lifestyles that destroy our individual and communal life. We starve both spirit and body with multiple addictions made possible by prosperity. We sustain addictions through economic policies that destroy our environmental life-support system. Through all of this we shake our heads at a suicide rate that has remained constant for generations, develop underfunded social policies to stop suicide, and make suicidal intent a condition for mandatory hospitalization.

18

Pastoral care of suicide takes place within this historical, religious, and contemporary matrix. Ministry in a context where suicide is either contemplated or completed is always difficult, emotionally draining, and sometimes dangerous. It raises multiple questions: How should suicide be interpreted to those at risk, to survivors, or to congregations? What resources and responsibilities do pastors have when facing suicide in the parish? Are there any effective answers for survivors who need comfort and explanation? Are there ways to prevent suicide in the parish? Over the past fifty years, research has shown that suicidal behavior is never simple. It is a complicated, multidimensional behavior with biological, psychological, social, and spiritual factors. My hope is that the following chapters will provide practical and thoughtful resources to equip pastors for this difficult ministry.

1

Assessing Suicide Potential in the Parish

S uicidal thoughts are part of normal human experience. Researchers estimate that nearly 25 percent of the U.S. population has at some point seriously considered ending their own lives. This same literature shows that about one-third of people who seek counseling have contemplated suicide,[1] and about 10 percent of all children and adolescents have at some time considered killing themselves.[2] These figures do not include people who have brief episodes when suicide crosses their mind or angry children who think about punishing parents with their death. Neither do they include temporarily distressed teens who impulsively blurt that they want to die or adults who have fleeting images of stress relieved by death. Images of death-within-life are so universal that Sigmund Freud wrote of a "death principle" that was fundamental to all human motivation. Within the stress of striving for rich life, there is a human factor that also pulls us to the silence of death. Freud believed this innate force explained suicidal thoughts, behavior, and self-destructive acts by individuals and society. Whether or not we accept Freud's analysis of human motivation, religious leaders can assume that many people in their congregations have self-destructive thoughts. Individuals under stress are likely to think about suicide, at least temporarily. Those with psychiatric illnesses, especially mood disorders such as major depression or bipolar disorder, may consider suicide forcefully.

Though suicidal thoughts are nearly universal, Christian history includes a strong suicide taboo. Too often, parishioners interpret this theological tradition of "the unpardonable sin" as condemnation of suicidal ideas over which they may have little control. Self-destructive thought symbolizes spiritual failure. For many committed Christians, this means never giving voice to such out-of-bounds thought in the general discourse of religious life. Suicidal thoughts, impulses, and intentions may lie carefully hidden behind a veil of religious propriety. It is not unusual for a pastor, church members, friends, and family to be completely surprised by a suicide or suicide attempt within the congregation. Strongly religious people may vigorously deny suicidal thoughts and resist disclosing the depth of their despair. It is fair for pastors to assume that at any given time there are people in their care who are considering suicide but are reluctant to disclose their feelings for fear of judgment. Good pastoral care requires that pastors develop nonthreatening ways to ask about depression and suicidal thoughts, assess suicide potential, establish an appropriate pastoral plan for intervention, and implement that plan.

While parish pastors usually are not trained as pastoral counselors, most have both the opportunity and the skills needed to evaluate suicide potential and make an appropriate judgment about intervention. Pastors often ask parishioners a variant of "how is life going?" When pastors are tuned to the fact that many depressed people reside in their congregation, answers to this question become more than a social cliché. Responses are data that give important clues. Good listening requires hearing at two levels—the words people say and the emotional frame, voice tone, facial expressions, and body postures that tell us how to receive another's words. At the first level, pastors need to be alert for a subtle suggestion that a person is in distress—such as "It's been a tough month"; "I could use a prayer"—and direct or humorous reference to ongoing sadness, unmanageable stress, hopelessness, or thoughts about dying. Equally important are nonverbal cues that make a socially appropriate response emotionally unbelievable. "I'm fine, thanks for asking" is incongruent with no eye contact, sad demeanor, soft voice, and a recent history of withdrawal from other social contact. In either case, follow-up conversation can open the door to disclose suicidal thinking.

Pastors who become skilled in assessing suicide potential must become comfortable with asking well-formed, non-threatening questions about depressive symptoms and learn to administer simple depression screening tools. Competence means dismissing the myth that asking about suicidal thoughts *suggests* suicide to depressed persons. There is no evidence that asking about suicide stimulates suicidal thinking. In fact, direct questions about suicide often free people to voice suicidal fears or talk about a plan to end their life for the first time. Most pastors can complete a three-step suicide assessment through a carefully constructed pastoral conversation. This requires preparation—thinking through and writing out a series of questions that will elicit responses about depression, risk factors, and the content of suicidal thoughts. It also requires a safe place for talking that is conducive to self-disclosure and expression of emotion.

ASSESSMENT PROCEDURES

Step One: Identifying Symptoms of Depression

A number of effective depression screening tools are available online without cost to pastors and other professionals.[3] These instruments are relatively simple. Most are designed to help health-care professionals identify and measure depressive symptoms. Some require special training to evaluate physical or mental functioning and may not be appropriate for pastoral contexts. When choosing a screening tool, pastors should determine whether special certification is required to use the instrument and whether they have sufficient training to evaluate the items required to complete the screening process. Publishers usually outline needed qualifications for using instruments. In some cases, consultation or supervision with a pastoral counselor or other mental health professional can provide the training needed to use these instruments appropriately and ethically.

In most pastoral contexts, simple questions about central symptoms of depression will provide enough information to determine if further assessment is necessary. In its initiative to help physicians and other primary care providers identify depressed individuals, the World Health Organization has provided a set of ten focused questions[4] that can be easily adapted to parish contexts. These are drawn from international diagnostic manuals (International Classification of Diseases-10, Diagnostic and Statistical Manual of Mental Disorders-IV). Potentially depressed people are asked: In the past two weeks, to what extent have you experienced: (1) Sadness and low spirits, (2) Loss of interest in daily activities, (3) Lack of energy or strength, (4) Loss of self-confidence, (5) Feelings of guilt or bad conscience, (6) Feelings that life is not worth living, (7) Difficulty concentrating on normal activities—such as reading, watching TV, (8) Restless or subdued feelings, (9) Trouble sleeping at night, (10) Reduced or increased appetite.

Symptoms are rated on a five-point scale. Scores of 1 mean the symptom has not been present, while a score of 5 indicates the symptom is always present. A 3 is scored if a symptom is present about half the time. Clinical diagnosis of depression must be left to certified pastoral counselors or other mental health and medical professionals. However, pastors have good reason to suspect depression and make appropriate referrals if a parishioner reports two or more of these items present more than half the time over a two-week period. Since suicide is directly related to feelings of hopelessness and depression, positive depression scores always warrant an assessment of suicide risk.

Step Two: Evaluating Suicide Risk Factors

About two-thirds of people who take their own life are depressed at the time of their death. At the same time, most depressed people do not harm themselves. While predicting suicide is complex and imprecise, researchers have identified a number of factors that make a suicide attempt more likely. Understanding the following risk factors can help pastors make appropriate decisions about intervention with depressed parishioners.

Men are at higher risk than women. European-American men and women account for more than 90 percent of all suicides in the United States.[5] Large-scale studies by the National Center for Health Statistics[6] show that European-American men account for nearly 75 percent of all suicides. Men complete suicide at a rate four to five times higher than women, and European-American men are twice as likely as men of other racial and ethnic groups to take their own life. This observation is age related. Demographic data shows a linear increase in suicide among European-American men beginning in early middle age. The older a man gets, the more likely he is to take his own life and the less likely he is to confess suicidal thoughts. These men tend to use extremely lethal means to end their life without warning.

High levels of hopelessness are directly related to suicidal action and may be more significant than high levels of depression. Depressive symptoms interact strongly with suicidal behavior, but alone they do not predict self-destructive behavior. Instead, depressive symptoms exacerbate feelings of hopelessness, stimulate social isolation, and impede thinking and judgment.

It is important for pastors to find ways to directly discuss, identify, and attend to feelings of hopelessness. This may be a challenge. As carers, our tendency is to project hope and to reassure a parishioner that all is not lost. It is easy to point to hopeful Scripture and God's ability to overcome all human circumstances. However, hopeless people often hear such encouragement as patronizing, evidence that they have failed in their personal and spiritual lives, or confirmation that not even God understands the depth of their feelings. This can result in emotional withdrawal, intensified resolve to end one's life, or a decision to placate a caring pastor with falsely manufactured pseudo-hope. The psalter is filled with evidence that hope is elusive without first plumbing the depths of despair. Nevertheless, this can be hard for pastors who have little time for sitting with depressed people or whose own sense of well-being is challenged by another's despair. Staring into the abyss with a parishioner can be overwhelming; exploring together what fearsome creatures inhabit the depths can be terrifying. It is much easier to recite that "all things work together for good for those who love God" (Rom. 8:28) and promise prayer from a distance than to share the weight of a blind gaze that sees no future.

When assessing suicide risk, pastors must connect emotionally with a depressed person's experience of hopelessness, speak directly to these feelings as real and understandable, and avoid any hint of easily hopeful solutions. Almost universally, hopelessly depressed people have tried and failed any solution a pastor can offer. Pastors must learn to engage hopelessness without inadvertently complicating the experience.

A history of alcohol or drug abuse is a strong risk factor for potential suicide. Toxicological studies show that more than half of those who complete suicide were legally intoxicated at the time of death.[7] In fact, alcoholism may be the strongest single predictor of completed suicide.[8] One group of researchers found that alcohol-dependent men may be twenty-five times more likely to kill themselves than the general population.[9] The combination of intense stress, interpersonal disruption, loss of support, and alcohol appears to be a deadly combination for men. Men in these circumstances are much more likely to attempt suicide using highly lethal and violent means (firearms, hanging) than the general population or their female counterparts. Studies show that alcohol produces a form of myopia that reduces an individual's perception and range of thinking. Intoxicated people are unable to think beyond preoccupation with immediate experience, are unlikely to consider the effects of their actions, and cannot see exceptions evident to others. This effect makes it easier to carry out suicidal acts.[10]

Recent loss of social support increases suicide risk. Such losses may include moving away from familiar friends and family, death of supportive persons, loss of church relationships, or social isolation resulting from depression. For men, divorce or death of a spouse may shatter social support systems.

Recent loss of employment or socioeconomic status increases suicide potential, particularly for men. Most often, this factor is associated with a sense of hopelessness about regaining what has been lost.

A depressed person with a family history of suicide is at increased risk. Completed suicides within families can model permission to take one's own life and offer death as a viable option to a hopeless situation. Family suicides may also activate long-term, complicated grief processes that erode transmission of hope within and across generations.

An individual diagnosed with a psychiatric illness is more likely to act on suicidal thoughts or impulses. Highest risks are related to affective disorders (such as major depression, bipolar disorder), thought disorders (such as schizophrenia or schizoaffective disorder), and some personality disorders.[11]

Additional risk factors include:

- Persons (especially men) who are widowed, divorced, or single;
- Persons with chronic physical illnesses;
- Persons experiencing intense, immediate emotional upheaval about family or personal matters;
- Previous suicide attempts;
- Individuals with access to firearms.

Risk factors do not mean that suicide is inevitable or that immediate action is warranted. They can (and should) heighten awareness for pastors who identify both depression and risk factors during an episode of care. Some factors are more important than others in certain situations. For instance, a depressed Euro American male parishioner who expresses hopelessness, has a history of alcohol abuse, and hunts regularly (and so has access to and comfort with firearms) presents a different constellation of risk than a depressed African American woman who is recently divorced, expresses hopelessness, and has good relational support. Understanding risk factors provides essential information for assessing the lethal potential of a depressed parishioner.

Step Three: Assessing Lethality

When depression and risk factors are present, lethality assessment is required. This usually includes evaluation of *suicidal intent* and *potential means*. Identifying *intent* involves exploring suicidal volition—the extent to which a person is invested in ending his or her life. Evaluating *means* questions the lethality of *how* an individual expects to die. Suicidal intent can be measured in three stages—thought only, identifiable plan, and timetable. Each stage requires careful investigation.

Stage One: Identifying Suicidal Thoughts. Thoughts about suicide can be observed on a continuum ranging from occasional intrusive images of death to continuous preoccupation with ending life as the only solution to a hopeless problem. At one end of the continuum, occasional thoughts of death may signal emotional distress but may not mark a significant risk for suicide. As thoughts of self-harm become more specific, the potential for self-harm increases.

A series of open-ended questions gives parishioners permission to talk about thoughts of self-harm and helps pastors evaluate the level of suicide intent. Because questions about depression and suicide are highly sensitive, they should be asked only in a context that can guarantee confidentiality and contain expression of intense feelings. This eliminates any public location or any situation in which a conversation could not be extended because of other commitments or priorities. Nonverbal cues such as glancing at a watch, answering a telephone, or looking toward an unfinished sermon on a computer can convey that conversation about depression is an unwanted intrusion. Questions about suicide or depression should always be limited to one-to-one pastoral conversation unless it is absolutely certain that a spouse or close friend is trusted, concerned, supportive, and will promote openness.

How questions about suicidal thinking are asked is also critical. Honesty will be short-circuited by subtle subtexts unconsciously communicated in pastoral conversation. Suicidal people will hesitate to self-reveal if they sense they will be subject to religious judgment or "chicken-soup" spiritualized responses. If parishioners perceive that their pastor is uncomfortable or inexperienced with deep emotional experience, they may choose to protect her or him from the darker side of life by keeping their suicidal thoughts to themselves. These factors require conscious attention to how pastors present themselves when asking sensitive questions about suicide. Rehearsing important questions about suicide with a sensitive partner can provide feedback about how critical questions are delivered and received. Practice can also create comfort talking about suicide.

Suicidal thoughts can be evaluated using several critical questions. "Have you considered harming yourself?" opens the door to talk about suicide. Asked in a nonthreatening, nonjudgmental way, this question gives permission to admit unacceptable suicidal thoughts gradually. Initial responses to "Have you considered harming yourself?" can be explored in more depth by using conversation encouragers. Nonverbal expressions of empathy (nods, facial expressions reflecting care), verbal reassurances ("I know how hard it is to talk about these thoughts"), encouragement to reveal more ("Can you tell me a little more about . . . ?"), and gradually more specific questions about suicidal ideas ("When you say you thought about the peace of dying, did you mean you were thinking about taking your own life?") will elicit important details for evaluation.

"How often do these thoughts occur to you?" is a critical question to evaluate how suicidal thoughts are intruding on everyday life. Since thoughts of self-harm are laden with ambivalent emotion, this question requires persistence and attention to detail. Good evaluation requires careful clarification of how often, when, and under what circumstances a depressed person considers suicide. This usually means asking more specific questions, such as: "Do you have thoughts of ending your life every day (or several times per week, etc.)?" "Do these thoughts come to you at particular times during the day?" "Do these thoughts occur to you in any particular circumstance, such as at work, at home, or at church?" "Are these thoughts related to any particular relationship in your life?" Specific questions can help determine how pervasive suicidal thinking has become—is it really "there all the time" or "just an occasional thought"? Suicide risk increases with frequency and specificity of suicidal thought. Well-formed, daily preoccupation with taking one's own life is more likely to become suicidal action than vague thoughts or death fantasies that emerge under stress. Talking about specific circumstances where suicidal thoughts increase can help pastors identify well-formed thoughts and clarify special circumstances that intensify despair. For instance, a person who thinks seriously of ending his or her life each Christmas does not pose as great a risk as one who considers suicide with each marital argument or each day of work. Persons for whom despair is pervasive and who consider ending their lives daily, regardless of changing circumstances, are at great risk.

"How do you feel about these thoughts?" This question helps to assess ambivalence about suicide. Most people who consider taking their own lives would like another option. Many are terrified by intrusive thoughts of suicide. A few are absolutely intent on removing themselves from the world. Pastors can probe carefully for feelings about death and beliefs about what death would accomplish. During assessment, it is important that parishioners feel that the depth of their experience is taken seriously. The agenda for this conversation is to help a suicidal person talk about feelings, fears, and beliefs that motivate his or her desire to die. This is not the place to correct untenable religious beliefs surrounding suicidal thinking. Neither is it the time to encourage a depressed person to feel differently about life. Such pressure to change will undermine self-revelation. Honest conversation often increases ambivalence about suicide, which can reduce the pressure of hopelessness. Careful probing can also reveal how comfortable a person is with the idea of ending life and how firmly committed they are to such action. People for whom death is a clear, acceptable solution to end hopelessness are at higher risk than those who are ambivalent or frightened about the prospect of ending their lives.

Stage Two: Identifiable Plan. Suicide potential increases dramatically if thoughts of harming one's self include a coherent idea of how life will end. Assessing a suicide plan requires a specific question: "Have you thought about how you will end your life?" As with previous questions, this must be asked with great care. It must be a sensitive invitation to share personal information that perhaps no one else in the world knows. It must also be timed well. A well-managed pastoral conversation will grant some "breathing time" during which a parishioner can gain comfort with disclosing forbidden thoughts to the pastor. Sitting with the reality of disclosure for a few minutes can reassure a parishioner that the pastor appreciates the depth of feelings, will not respond reactively by trying to talk him or her out of suicidal thoughts, and will not abandon the person emotionally in the most serious conflict of their life.

31

Disclosure of a suicide plan requires careful, active listening that must accomplish several things at once. First, good listening should reassure the speaker that the pastor is not making negative judgments and will not react impulsively by prematurely notifying family members or authorities. Second, good listening must enhance trust that may later be needed for intervention. Finally, good listening must encourage self-disclosure of intimate details of a suicide plan. The following questions, in one form or another, should be posed and answered:

- How do you plan to end your life?
- What means will you use?
- Where will this take place?
- When will you carry out this plan?

In the end, careful listening is meant to draw out specific details of any plan for self-harm and establish an empathic connection that will facilitate intervention.

A person who has mentally organized the steps needed to end life has already made significant progress toward lethal action. The simple fact that suicidal thoughts have progressed to the planning stage is enough to require direct pastoral action. However, details are important to assess what level of intervention is required. Plans can be evaluated on these dimensions:

1. How specific is the plan? Serious suicide plans often include selection of a method for ending life, a decision about the conditions under which the action will be taken, managing "good-byes," and a timetable. Often, planning will include care for managing the aftermath of death. Well-formed plans require hours of thought and considerable emotional energy. Planning allows a suicidal individual cognitive space and emotional time to gain comfort with death and suicidal action. Very specific, detailed plans communicate a high level of intent.

In some cases, pastors may need to account for people they know to be impulsive. These people may not construct detailed plans, but instead make taking their life contingent upon specific circumstances, such as job failure or intensified marital conflict. In these cases, pastors need to evaluate how clearly circumstances are described and what contingencies are central to a suicide plan.

2. *How "doable" is the plan?* Plans that are immediately available are higher risk than plans requiring specific conditions not immediately present. For example, one client in pastoral counseling revealed a well-considered plan to drive his car to a secluded area outside town, sit one last time to watch the sun rise, and then end his life with a shotgun he kept in his trunk always loaded. He had set no date, but awoke each morning preoccupied with dying that day. A second client planned to drive his car from a high bridge over the Pacific Ocean. However, he did not presently own a car and lived a two-day drive inland from the bridge he had selected. He did have a vague plan of how he would acquire a car. He also reported several important details needing resolution prior to ending his life.

The first example is very high risk. The plan is clear and precise. The location has been set, conditions affirmed, and the means of suicide are immediately available. The second example is a lower risk. Details are not clearly thought through, conditions have yet to be met for action, and the means are not immediately available. Both cases require intervention. The first will require immediate action.

3. *How lethal or violent is the plan?* A plan for a violent end often reflects determination to die. Plans that include firearms, hanging, and jumping from high structures represent the highest potential for completed suicide. These methods leave little room for second thoughts or unforeseen intervention. Studies show that owning a firearm presents the highest risk of lethality. Firearms are one of the most certain and violent ways to bring life to an end and usually require no delay. A plan to end life less violently often requires time to gather

medications, to travel, or to construct some apparatus to die. Delay allows last-minute rethinking, chance intervention, or failure of the selected methods.

Access to firearms requires immediate intervention. However, under no circumstances should a pastor try to intervene personally when firearms are present. In several instances, pastors trying to talk suicidal parishioners away from their weapon have become victims of homicide-suicide or have been shot accidentally as parishioners ended their own life. It is reckless to put oneself or another at risk with a loaded weapon present. If loaded weapons are part of an immediate suicide plan or threat, calling the police is the only responsible alternative. Making a call to the police does not end a pastor's role in intervention. Many communities and police departments value pastors' skills and presence when managing suicide emergencies. Pastors can be available for follow-up care and in some instances can be included in a team managing a firearm crisis.

4. *Are alcohol or drugs involved in the plan?* More than half of all suicides are completed by persons who are legally intoxicated. Alcohol facilitates suicidal thinking, removes final barriers to suicidal action, and escalates risk.

5. *Has the suicidal person set a date and time for death?* An individual who has set a concrete date for his or her death is at high risk, particularly if the date is in the immediate future.

6. *Has the person finalized conditions for the plan?* Suicidal people who have organized conditions for their death are at extremely high risk. Those most at risk may not reveal that they are preparing for death. This may require pastors to ask others whether a suicidal individual has set personal affairs in order, changed a will, suddenly paid off debts, arranged for a funeral, or behaved in any way that could be seen as "saying good-bye." Since finalizing plans for death can energize a severely depressed person, pastors should question sudden positive mood changes such as incongruent cheerfulness, remarkable increases in energy, or episodes of unusual productivity.

7. *Is there evidence of impulsivity?* Momentary impulses can result in lethal action. Assessment should include a question like: "*Have you had sudden impulses to harm yourself that were hard to control?*" Follow-up conversation can then explore how impulses in other areas of life—such as spending, alcohol consumption, or relationships—have been managed. People with a history of poor impulse control or whose control has been compromised by depression may be at high risk without a clear or viable plan. It is especially important to note any recent problems in impulse control.

Jane presented symptoms of depression and hopelessness. She occasionally thought of ending her life, but had no clear plan. In one conversation, Jane reported that she had been to several clubs and could not stop drinking. She had sex with a man she did not know, thinking, "What do I have to lose?" The following morning she was overwhelmed with remorse and self-hate and wished she had enough drugs to kill herself. Careful questions revealed that Jane often had trouble controlling binge spending and could be mercurial in beginning and ending romantic relationships. She had worked hard over several years to manage her impulsivity, but recently found her control slipping.

In cases where impulsivity is an issue, a pastoral plan must include action to safeguard against spontaneous suicide. This may include notifying a spouse, relative, or close friend to check regularly on impulsive thinking and constructing a no-suicide contract that helps regulate sudden action through accountability. (No-suicide contracts are discussed later in this chapter.)

8. *Has reality testing or mental functioning been impaired by depression or hopelessness?* Suicide risk increases dramatically when people are cognitively impaired. Pastors may notice that a depressed person is "not thinking straight" or perceives reality in a markedly unusual way. Careful observation and clarifying questions can provide enough information to inform action. For instance, cognitively impaired people may report that they feel unable to keep their thoughts

in order. *(Clarifying question: "Can you tell me what you mean when you say 'I can't keep track of my mind'?")* Some may speak in ways that confuse listeners because they cannot maintain a coherent line of thought or because the subject matter makes no rational sense. *(Observation: No matter what clarifying questions are asked, the conversation still does not make sense.)* Impairment may include delusions,* hallucinations, or a sense that others (or God) are controlling their thought or behavior. *(Clarifying questions: "Can you explain what you mean when you say you are responsible for . . . ?" "When you say you hear God speaking to you, what do you mean?" "Tell me a little more about how John, your coworker, made you drive your car off the road." Observations: Odd behaviors that might suggest listening to sounds or seeing something not in the interview room.)* Impaired people may also be disoriented in time and place—they may not know where they are, why they are in the pastor's office, what day or time it is, or the name of the city or state in which they reside. *(Clarifying questions: "Why did you come in to see me today?" "Why am I here to visit you?" "What day/month/year is today?" "Where do you live?")* Recent loss of memory or ability to perform typical mental tasks may also point to cognitive impairment. These symptoms are not uncommon in seriously depressed people and demand immediate psychiatric consultation. If a psychiatrist is not immediately available for a telephone consultation, facilitating a trip to a hospital emergency room is a first pastoral priority.

Stage 3. Timetable. Assessing a timetable requires asking a suicidal person concrete questions about what steps will lead to death and what progress has been made toward that end. Conversation about a suicide timetable is sensitive. It

---

*A delusion is a mistaken belief about everyday life that most unimpaired people know to be in error, such as "I'm being watched by the CIA," grandiose beliefs of controlling others, or convictions of one's own horrific sin that exceeds all boundaries of religious faith or rationality.

requires deep understanding of the parishioner's hopelessness and empathic connection to his or her desire to end life. This connection makes it possible for a person thinking forbidden thoughts to reveal action they have taken toward a taboo. This conversation must convey that the pastor understands, is not judgmental, and will accept what is revealed without panic or overreaction. (*"You have obviously thought deeply about taking your own life. I've heard you say that suicide feels like the only option you have. You have considered what death will mean to you and those around you. You also told me that you have decided how you will take your own life. You already have what it takes to end your life—own a gun, have collected the pills, purchased the rope, etc.—Can you tell me what is left to do before you carry out your plan?"*)

Plan and timetable reflect the level of intent, lethality, and immediacy of concern. For instance, the client described above with a shotgun in his trunk confessed that he had taken care of his financial affairs, had said good-bye to the important people in his life, and had given away his most important possessions. He had purchased a bottle of his favorite bourbon and was simply awaiting tomorrow's rising sun. He was at extreme risk. His intent was clear, his plan concrete, and his timetable complete. Direct and immediate intervention was required. But, the client with an incomplete plan who intended to drive from a bridge required serious attention but no immediate crisis intervention. Risk of immediate harm is considerably lower in the second case and allows more options for pastoral response.

Every suicidal thought should be taken seriously without overreaction. Each case is unique and requires careful, individual assessment. This relies largely on a pastor's ability to form a trusting, conversational relationship with a suicidal person that reduces shame and fear of judgment. Accurate empathic understanding of a suicidal person's experience facilitates disclosure and makes intervention possible.

DEVELOPING A PLAN FOR INTERVENTION

Any time a person discloses suicidal thoughts or intent to a pastor, some form of intervention is required. In some situations, this may be as simple as a careful follow-up conversation that clarifies low suicide risk. It may also be as complex as immediately mobilizing family, police, and emergency medical services to stop an imminent, violent suicide. It is useful to organize intervention around three levels of risk management.

Low-Risk Intervention

Low-risk interventions can be used when assessment shows little evidence of significant depression, few risk factors, and suicidal thoughts that are occasional without a formed plan. The following case illustrates evaluation procedures and a low-risk intervention plan.

James

James is a fifty-seven-year-old male. He has been married for eighteen years to Carol. Both were married previously. He and his wife have four children from previous marriages and one child born to them. Two of their five children are in college. James has frequently expressed satisfaction that all his children will have the advantage of a college education. James was a team leader in a small steel fabricating business for twenty years. He enjoyed his work and saw himself as a highly dependable and valuable employee. James's wife is a secretary for the public school system. The couple have been important lay leaders in their small church. James served several terms as chair of the board.

Pastor Brown met with James to discuss details of a church fund-raising program. During their conversation, James confided that he was uncertain about his own future. His company had been sold to a large international consortium and his job was eliminated as unnecessary. The new owners offered no severance apart from one-month notification. After two months of looking for other options, James had concluded that his qualifications and age did not meet the needs of the contemporary job market. He felt helpless. His retirement funds were meager. Furthermore, he had borrowed against them and the equity in his house to pay college tuition. He was concerned about how he would keep his children in college and meet his financial obligations. He joked that he was worth more dead than alive. He had good life insurance. His family would be able to get financial aid without him around.

Following the meeting, Pastor Brown was troubled by James's jest about being worth more dead than alive. Though he did not know James well, it seemed that he had been working hard to appear cheerful. Recently he had uncharacteristically missed a number of church meetings, reporting later that he did not feel well. Pastor Brown scheduled a pastoral call with James the following day. He prepared for a conversation through which he could evaluate possible depression, risk factors, and suicidal ideation.

In the first few minutes of conversation, Pastor Brown established a relational connection with James by discussing recent family and church events. This connection allowed Pastor Brown to comment:

"James, yesterday I couldn't help hearing how hard losing your job has been. It sounds like it's becoming a serious situation."

James: "It's been very hard. I couldn't believe this happened. It took me a week to feel like it was real. Then I thought, 'No big deal, I've found jobs before.' Trouble is, last time I looked for a job I was in my thirties. I know two months isn't a long time, but it seems like forever. No money coming in, kids in college, and no response to any of my job applications. For a while I called the personnel offices back, but the answer was always the same. No jobs available. I don't have training for high-tech jobs. My experience makes me overqualified for entry-level jobs. It's hard to hear that time after time."

Pastor: "It sounds like the weight of all this is starting to pull you down."

James: "Yes, it is."

Pastor: "James, can I ask you some pretty direct questions about how all of this is affecting you?"

James: "Sure, just as long as you don't tell me I'm crazy or ask for money."

(Depression assessment)

Pastor: "I'm glad to see you're keeping a sense of humor in all this. (pause) Humor is good, but yesterday I had the sense you were feeling pretty low and sad." (question 1, depression assessment)

James: "Yeah, at times when I think about all this I get pretty low and I don't feel like doing anything."

(Response leads to question 2, depression assessment)

Pastor: "On a scale of one to five, where one is low and sad all the time and five is never low and sad, where do you think you fit over the past two weeks?"

James: "I think I'd have to say I'm pretty much at a three right now. I don't think about this all the time or anything, but when I do I get pretty low."

Pastor: "You said just a second ago that you don't feel like doing much. How often has that happened for you in the past two weeks?" (question 3, depression assessment)

James: "It's not all the time. Some days I get up and get really motivated. Then I run into this brick wall and I can't do anything. I guess maybe a third of the time I just feel too tired to do anything. In those times I feel like 'why bother? I don't have anything anybody wants anyway.'"

(Leads in to question 4, depression assessment).

Pastor: "So on a scale of 1 to 5, you would say this happens about . . ."

James: "I guess about a two."

Conversational questions continue with Pastor Brown leading toward responses to the ten questions of depression assessment.

Following the protocol for depression screening, Pastor Brown observes that James reports:

1. Sadness and low spirits (3)
2. Loss of interest in daily activities (2)
3. Lack of energy or strength (2)
4. Loss of self-confidence (3)
5. Feelings of guilt or bad conscience (1)
6. Feelings that life is not worth living (2)
7. Difficulty concentrating on normal activities (3)
8. Restless or subdued feelings (2)
9. Trouble sleeping at night (3)
10. Reduced or increased appetite (1)

With these scores, Pastor Brown concludes that depressive symptoms are not pervasive enough to take immediate action for intervention. However, James is clearly experiencing a period of low morale. It is clear that the loss of his job has resulted in some sadness and some fear. He reported that his situation keeps him awake at nights thinking about half the time. However, he does not think this is a problem. Historically he often lies awake "when things bother" him. At this time, sleeplessness is not regular enough to diminish James's ability to think or function.

Based on what he already knows about James and adding a few focused questions, Pastor Brown can assess suicide risk. He knows that James is a middle-aged or older male, a category that represents most completed suicides. He also fits another risk category—he has recently lost his job and his socioeconomic status is threatened. He is experiencing a period of stress and emotional upheaval but appears to be managing this with his current support systems and usual coping mechanisms. He does not report feeling out of control. Furthermore, his social systems are intact. He is married and physically healthy. Assessing hopelessness requires sensitivity on Pastor Brown's part. When James said he felt that life was not worth living at times, Pastor Brown spent several minutes talking with James about his sense of hope and hopelessness. While James is feeling a bit helpless in his current circumstance, he also asserted a sense of hope about the future and training for a new career. He also saw his relationship with God, his family, and his church as central to his trust in the future. In James's own assessment, all is not lost. He sees possibilities he has not yet explored, though this will take energy he is not sure he has.

Pastor Brown was also careful to ask about alcohol. James reported no change in drinking. He has one or two beers with his friends once or twice a month. He has no history of alcohol problems. Pastor Brown knows of no psychiatric history, and when asked, James reported he had never been treated for depression or other emotional problems.

Since Pastor Brown heard James make a specific reference to the benefits of his death, it is essential that Pastor Brown follow up specifically with questions about suicide.

Pastor: "James, yesterday you said you were worth more dead than alive. Today you said sometimes you felt life was not worth living. Have you considered harming yourself?"

James: "The thought has crossed my mind a time or two. Killing myself would give my wife and kids the money they need. But, I know that's crazy thinking."

Pastor: "How often do you think about this?"

James: "Really, it was just a quick thought a time or two. I know that's not an answer. I want to live. I don't want to die, I want to see my grandkids." (Response clarifies that suicidal thoughts are transient and not well-formed. It also contains an expression of hope.)

Pastor: "Have you thought about how you would take your own life?"

James: "No, not at all. I just thought I would have to do it some way that wasn't obvious so it doesn't cancel my life insurance. Like I said, I want to live. I guess I really believe we'll get out of this mess one way or another."

With these responses, Pastor Brown can conclude that James has had momentary thoughts of harming himself but has not formulated a plan or timetable. His reasoning is intact and appears appropriate. He does not appear impulsive. His image of how he would take his own life is vague, and he has not alluded to violent, or certainly, lethal means to end his life. Intent appears very low or absent. This gives Pastor Brown considerable flexibility in his response to James.

Low suicide risk allows a variety of care plans. Referral to a pastoral counselor or other mental health professional may be appropriate but may not be necessary. Many parishioners may rightly believe they can manage their distress without formal therapeutic intervention. Good pastoral care will help parishioners assess the benefits and liabilities of therapy. Whether or not a parishioner is referred to a therapist, pastoral care in the parish continues.

A plan for care with a low-risk person like James will include several primary elements. First, a "no-suicide" agreement must be negotiated between pastor and parishioner. This can be a verbal agreement cast in the strongest language of covenant. It intends to hold a parishioner accountable to their pastor: (*"As part of our relationship, I need for us to make an agreement. I care about whether you live or die. I am concerned about your suicidal thoughts. I need an absolute agreement from you that you will take no action to harm yourself without first talking with me face-to-face. I also need your promise that you will contact me and talk with me if you begin to feel overwhelmed by feelings that you want to end your life. I also need your promise that if you are physically unable to contact me and cannot control your feelings, you will immediately go to a hospital emergency room and get help."*) This covenant is central to any care plan when suicidal thoughts are present. It is the first order of business and must be reinforced regularly. During times of crisis, a no-suicide contract may be revisited daily or weekly.

Lower risk requires less frequent reinforcement. Simple questions, such as *"How are you managing things today/this week?"* or *"How are you doing with our agreement?"* can focus a conversation on the contract.

No-suicide contracts can relieve depressed people of some of the pressure of making an immediate decision. The contract sets an intermediate condition that makes action less likely. It also communicates that at least one important person cares enough to change his or her own daily routine to preserve the person's life. For people who may act impulsively, accountability to a pastor, particularly within the context of an ongoing empathic relationship, may add just enough impulse control to rethink lethal action. If a parishioner is unwilling to make this covenant, a pastor must make an immediate referral to qualified mental health professionals or facilitate admission to a hospital.

Second, an adequate care plan will include a series of regular follow-up conversations initiated by the pastor: "I would like for us to meet once a week for a while so we can keep track of how you are managing this stressful time. Each time I'll probably ask you about your depressive feelings and thoughts about harming yourself." These meetings can be a time to reinforce a no-suicide contract and a simple opportunity to "check in" with each other. They can also be opportunities to make religious sense of a difficult time. For instance, conversations might include careful theological "wondering" and praying about what it means to be abandoned and rejected after years of service or what it means to feel the future at extreme risk. Together James and Pastor Brown might test the meaning of prayer that seems unanswered or specifically discuss spiritual practices that bring religious resources to bear on his circumstance. In these conversations, Pastor Brown will want to avoid easy theological answers or "chicken-soup" spiritual platitudes. These "easy answers" rarely provide the hope nondepressed people think they will. They often alienate a depressed person who cannot make the "magic" work. However, Pastor Brown will want to highlight times when James does not feel abandoned, rejected, or sad. He will want to notice when hope spontaneously appears in conversations, focus on how it suddenly "popped up," and consider with James how that might happen more regularly.

Third, Pastor Brown will want to help James sustain supportive congregational relationships at a time when his lack of energy and shame make this difficult. Together they can examine his participation in congregational life and decide what is most life-giving for him.

Fourth, pastoral planning will solidify James's network of support by including family members and close friends in the plan for intervention. Together James and Pastor Brown can discuss how and when his wife and good friends can be "brought on board" with the depth of his experience. This may include directly confronting James's shame about losing his job and not easily finding another.

Finally, Pastor Brown will want to maintain a consultative relationship with a pastoral counselor to discuss concerns or developments in James's case.

High-Risk Intervention

High-risk interventions are necessary when assessment shows a high level of depression, numerous risk factors, and high potential for lethality. The following case illustrates pastoral action in a high-risk situation.

Julie

Julie is a twenty-year-old unmarried college student who works part-time in a restaurant. Her grandmother, Caroline, called Pastor Anderson when Julie appeared at her door "an emotional wreck." Caroline was frightened by Julie's intense feelings and became more alarmed when Julie said she wished she could die. She was also frightened because Julie had been hospitalized at seventeen for a suicide attempt the family never talked about. Pastor Anderson rearranged her schedule to meet with Julie the same evening. During their conversation, Julie was sad and tearful. She said she felt ineffective in life. Her relationship of six months had ended in abuse. She had no place to live and was giving up hope of finding someone who could love her.

Julie described her life as "all downhill" since her early adolescence. Through high school she drank heavily, acted out sexually, and experimented with drugs. Julie had been involved in several intense relationships since her late teens, all ending when her partner became physically abusive. When guaranteed that Pastor Anderson would not tell her grandmother, Julie revealed her last two relationships were with lesbian partners. She stated that she had begun losing weight and admitted that she was cutting her arms—something she had not done since high school.

During the conversation, Pastor Anderson completed depression screening and found eight of ten symptoms of depression present all the time or most of the time. Risk assessment raised Pastor Anderson's concern. Julie reported a high level of hopelessness, a history of drug and alcohol abuse (Julie reported drinking heavily in the past two weeks), compromised family and social support system, high levels of emotional upheaval, a history of psychiatric treatment (Julie could not remember a diagnosis), and a previous suicide attempt. Pastor Anderson also knew that suicide rates in adolescents and young adults have increased dramatically and that three young adults had recently completed suicides on Julie's college campus. Communities often have episodes of suicide "contagion" resulting from one or more completed suicide deaths. These factors increased Julie's risk.

Lethality assessment revealed that Julie had been thinking seriously of taking her own life for several weeks. She had collected a number of prescription medications, researched their lethality, and carried them in her purse. Her plan was to drink as much alcohol as she could without losing consciousness, and then take her pills at home. She had set her plan in motion the previous evening and was well on her way to intoxication when her estranged partner unexpectedly returned. Julie became agitated, ran from her apartment, and went to her grandmother's house to sleep. Julie reported that she intends to complete her suicide as soon as she returns home. She can no longer face the struggle she lives daily.

Julie was demonstrating depression, hopelessness, and a number of significant risk factors. Most important, she had a specific and "doable" plan, the means to carry out her plan, and a definite (and immediate) timetable. Her reasoning and judgment were impaired by emotional upheaval, depression, impulsivity, lack of sleep, and alcohol. In this case, immediate action was required. Pastor Anderson's primary goal was to assure Julie's safety and mobilize community resources for her care. Unlike James's situation, Pastor Anderson's options with Julie were limited.

- If possible, Pastor Anderson must form an empathic connection with Julie and help her participate in securing her own safety. This will include taking the time to name her pain and affirm the depth of her distress. By forming an emotional connection to the depth of Julie's despair, Pastor Anderson may be able to avoid a battle of wills she cannot win when it is time to intervene. This connection will allow her to clarify Julie's suicidal intentions and outline needed action. "Julie, it's clear you intend to kill yourself. You and I need to do something about that. I want to make sure that doesn't happen today. Do you think we can find a way to keep you safe until you can look at all the options?" This response allows Julie to make decisions about her own safety and offers subtle hope. At the same time, her choice is limited to "today" so that she does not feel trapped by giving up her preferred option permanently.
- If Julie is willing to participate in her own care, she can be asked to relinquish the means of her death.

Since the pills are in Julie's purse, Pastor Anderson can ask to hold them for her. Suicidal individuals often form an intense attachment to the means of their death. This is not easily released. Julie may need reassurance that Pastor Anderson will not destroy the pills.

• Pastor Anderson's next step is to mobilize resources. Her first act will be to ask Julie's permission to invite her grandmother, or others emotionally close to Julie, into the conversation. "Julie, this is a difficult situation. I think it is important for you to have someone nearby that you trust. Can we invite your grandmother in? I think she can help with some decisions we need to make to keep you safe." Including important people in Julie's decision-making process can help her feel supported and agree to immediate medical care. If she refuses intervention, these same people can help facilitate involuntary care.

• At this point, pastoral conversation will affirm the depth of Julie's distress, the immediate danger she faces, and a statement that her only viable option is medical intervention. Unless Pastor Anderson has a psychiatric consultant upon whom she can call, she and other supportive family members will need to take Julie to a local hospital and help her through the process of emergency admission.

Special consideration 1. In managing suicidal crises, it is imperative that pastors not endanger their own or others' lives. Julie's case involves nonviolent suicidal means. Under no circumstances should a pastor try to take firearms or other weapons from suicidal persons. If a pastor suspects that weapons are present in a suicidal parishioner's home, conversations should take place in the pastor's office or another safe location. When weapons are present, the only responsible course of pastoral action is to call the police. At this point, pastors may become an important part of a team managing a serious suicide crisis.

Special consideration 2. Helping Julie through hospitalization may be time-consuming and vexing. Pastor Anderson will need to draw upon her knowledge of local health-care and emergency procedures. For instance, without a life-threatening suicide attempt in progress (actually ingesting pills), will local emergency rooms evaluate or admit her? If Julie does not have health insurance, where is her best chance for admission? Getting to know local procedures prior to a crisis will help Pastor Anderson advocate for Julie in a complex medical context.

Special consideration 3. If Julie is unwilling to act on her own behalf, Pastor Anderson may need to take steps for nonvoluntary admission. Depending on local policy, this may mean calling the police or Emergency Medical Services. It is important for pastors to know who (police, EMS) can initiate this action. It is helpful if pastors maintain a consultative relationship with a psychologist or social worker able to make nonvoluntary admissions. This can eliminate the stigma of an EMS or police admission.

Special consideration 4. It is possible that Julie will be refused emergency services. In this event, Pastor Anderson must rely on family and congregational resources. Family and friends must be recruited to assure that Julie is never alone and that she is separated from the means of death. Pastor Anderson will need to find psychiatric or psychological consultation for Julie within twenty-four hours. This will usually require intentional, insistent, and firm advocacy with family, friends, and professionals.

Hospitalization or professional referral does not end Pastor Anderson's responsibility. Like James in the earlier case study, Julie will need pastoral aftercare. In Julie's case, it is appropriate and necessary for Pastor Anderson to gain permission from Julie to consult often with her therapist so that her care can be coordinated. By including Julie's therapist, Pastor Anderson will be more effective in mobilizing necessary congregational resources and addressing religious and spiritual issues that arise from her experience.

The Intervention Continuum

James and Julie illustrate two ends of a continuum. Most often, assessment will reveal an intermediate level of risk needing two levels of response. The first response is to establish that pastoral presence is an act of intervention. This requires proactive engagement that asks specific questions, names stark realities, and establishes an ongoing covenant of accountability with parishioners. This covenant must begin with a "no-suicide" agreement and include a plan for regular conversations, ongoing spiritual care, and careful, continuous evaluation of suicidal intent. Second, intermediate risk usually requires immediate referral for counseling and medical evaluation. This is managed best when pastors maintain good working relationships with pastoral counselors or other mental health professionals in between crises. Parishioners are more likely to comply with referral when it is clear that the pastor knows and trusts the therapist. A pastor who sits with a depressed person and calls a therapist on this person's behalf sends several powerful messages. It affirms the pastor's prior relationship with the therapist and commitment to immediate and active intervention on behalf of the parishioner. It also symbolizes accountability and signals the therapist that the pastor will be engaged in ongoing care with this parishioner. All are important.

Referral is central to care but is not the whole of care. What happens *outside* of therapy has profound effects for depressed and suicidal people. *Pastoral care is not just an adjunct to psychotherapy or medical treatment. Pastors are primary care providers who make referrals to extend congregational care. Parishioners live their lives in communities and congregations, not in therapists' or physicians' offices.* This position means that it is the pastor's responsibility to stay in consultation with parishioners and therapists. A pastoral care plan for a suicidal individual must include regular follow-up with mental health professionals to whom referrals are made. Usually, this means arranging appropriate consent from parishioners so that interprofessional collaboration can take place. Consultation keeps the pastor aware of the client's progress and can inform care offered through the congregation. Pastors are important referral sources for many therapists and professional colleagues involved in ongoing care for those referred. Most competent therapists will welcome pastoral involvement in client cases with appropriate release from the client referred. Therapists who resist consultation may be inappropriate for pastoral referrals.

ABOUT DOCUMENTATION

Though pastors generally do not keep case files for care with parishioners, note keeping is important when suicide is an issue. Parish pastors have professional responsibilities and need to document that they have taken appropriate steps to safeguard those in their care. These notes need not be elaborate, but should include: (1) what caused the pastor concern, using quotes from the parishioner when possible, (2) steps taken to evaluate the problem, such as a summary of depression screening and lethality assessment, and (3) a summary of action taken for intervention, including any referral. Notes should always be dated. As with all care documents, these are confidential notes and must be secured in locked drawers or file cabinets.

SUMMARY: GUIDELINES AND DECISION TREE

Managing parishioners with suicidal thoughts and intent can be complex and time-consuming. The following guidelines are useful:

- Spend time learning about community resources before a crisis;
- Pastors should be prepared to spend intense, concentrated time managing a suicide crisis;

51

- Always take symptoms of depression, hopelessness, and any reference to death seriously;
- Always ask about suicidal thoughts. Remember—asking about suicide does not suggest suicide to people;
- Establish and maintain relationships with pastoral counselors and other professionals who can consult with you in a suicide crisis;
- Never, under any circumstances, try to intervene with a suicidal person who has access to a weapon or may become violent;
- Assume that every suicidal crisis, from low risk to high risk, will require ongoing pastoral care for persons involved;
- Use the Decision Tree (fig. 1) to assist in pastoral decision-making.

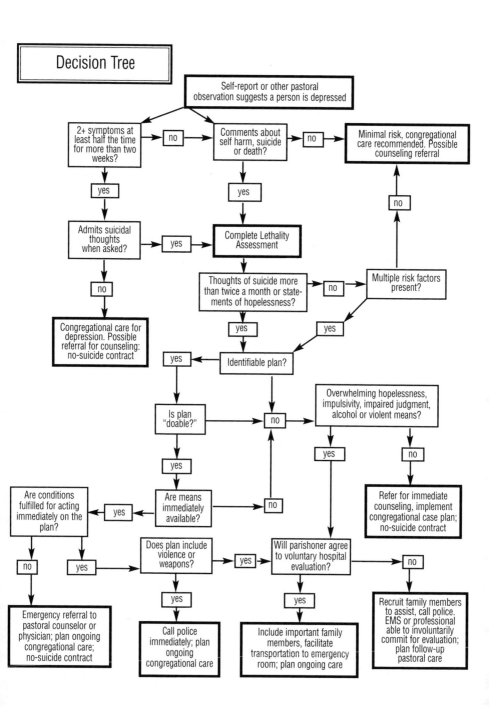

Figure 1

2

Suicide Attempts, Care, and Recovery

About 70 percent of those who successfully end their own life do so the first time they try. Nearly all white males (90 percent) die with their first attempt. At the same time, nonfatal suicide attempters far outnumber those who succeed by a ratio of at least 10 to 1 and possibly as high as 25 to 1.[1] The relationship between suicide attempts and completion is confusing. Posed one way, 30 percent of all persons who complete a suicide have made at least one previous attempt. Yet, when the data is examined closely, only 10 to 15 percent of those who fail at suicide succeed at a later date. In this light, pastors are far more likely to be confronted by a suicide attempt than a completed suicide.

Nonfatal suicide attempts are complex. Some attempts appear more serious than others. Motivation toward suicide may be unclear—did the person want to die or was this some form of cry for help? To what extent are apparent accidents, misuse of drugs and alcohol, or high-risk behavior forms of suicidal intent? Suicide specialists agree that an attempted suicide exists when a person injures himself or herself intentionally, but does not die.[2] This definition includes people who may be ambivalent about dying. It relieves the pressure to distinguish those who are "truly suicidal" and those who may make "suicidal gestures." Such a distinction is difficult to establish and may not mean much for treatment and recovery. In either case, people who have made one suicide attempt are at higher risk for completing suicide during their

55

lifetime than the general population. Perhaps the most significant part of this data is that survivors are available for intervention and in most cases intervention is effective.

Congregational care is an important part of intervention. To provide quality care, pastors must be familiar with common dynamics related to attempted suicide and have a conceptual frame for organizing care. My purpose in this chapter is:

- To illustrate dynamics often present for individuals, families, and communities following a person's attempt to end his or her own life. These examples are neither exhaustive nor paradigmatic. They are meant only to illustrate a pastoral process for looking carefully and closely at the context of a suicide attempt. It is less important for pastors to grasp all possible contingencies, probabilities, or psychological meanings of a suicide attempt than to have an informed method for constructing a system of response.
- To propose a model of pastoral reflection and intervention that can help re-form individual and community stories of self-harm in redemptive ways.

A FOUNDATION FOR CARE

People who fail in a suicide attempt face a world that demands rational reasons and intelligible explanations for behavior that is almost always irrational. Suicide can rarely be understood in conventional terms. Nevertheless, friends and family want the security of easily understandable answers. Unfortunately, most people who attempt suicide can offer no clear, unambiguous reason for their action. Such extreme action usually reflects deep pain that is not easily explained or easily managed. Were solutions as simple as nonsuicidal people believe, alternatives other than self-harm would have been chosen. When asked "why?" survivors may refuse to comment because their motives are likely to be misunderstood or because they do not clearly understand their own motives. Often, medical or psychotherapeutic professionals fill this void by ascribing motivation. It is noteworthy that people who survive a suicide attempt rarely agree with professionally determined descriptions of motivation.[3] Tensions in how a suicide attempt is interpreted can set a survivor at odds with loved ones and threaten important social relationships.

Many times, by the time one who has tried to end life meets with his or her pastor, a complex set of meanings and interactions have rearranged social relationships. Doctors have diagnosed. Motives have been evaluated through psychiatric and psychological frames. Family and friends have been instructed to act on professional opinions and recommendations. Survivors often have little control over how their experience is understood or how their life is reassigned to them after a nonfatal attempt. Clients often express feelings like the following:

> I'm not a daughter or a mother or a friend anymore. I am a "suicide risk," a new class of nonperson. People aren't with me; they watch me. They want answers I don't have, so they tell me what I felt and why I did what I did. I'm told my attempt was a power play in my marriage to get attention and manipulate. Like life and death are some kind of business deal. I'm told I didn't really want to die because I didn't do it right the first time. Don't get me wrong. I sincerely wanted to die, even though today I'm glad I wasn't thinking clearly enough to be sure I did it right. I'm finding some things to live for, but when you are a "suicide risk" nothing you say matters.

Pastors are in a unique position to help suicide attempters reconnect with life. Good pastoral care does not depend on uncovering true motivation or accepting a particular analysis of relational power dynamics. Instead, care is about restoring humanity and relationships. People who have made a suicide attempt must find their way back to God's table as legitimate human beings. They must find Christ's invitation through the haze of suspicion, recrimination, self-doubt, embarrassment, and, at times, self-loathing. Individual and family therapy will help but cannot replace the ministry of reconciliation as it is lived out in congregational care.

PASTORAL CARE:
A WAY OF CONNECTING WITH STORIES

Humans organize life and experience through narrative. We live our lives in a rich stew of multileveled, embedded stories that define our specific social location and set of meanings. Our identity is nestled in memory. Memory is structured largely by internalized past and present experiences given emotional meaning through shared social narratives. We are who we are largely because of stories constructed in relationship with others. We know where we fit in the world by how our personal set of stories fits with social, political, and religious narratives contained in the dominant culture. These narratives define "normal" and tell us what kind of thought, action, and relationships are acceptable and unacceptable. For instance, if our history, behavior, skin color, religious expression, and sexual orientation allow us to participate in normative cultural narratives, we feel accepted. We have access to privileges afforded by the power of the dominant cultural story; we share in decision-making and some control of the future. In the United States, this dominant narrative might partly be described as white, middle class, politically conservative or mainline liberal, heterosexual, successfully married or single by choice, generally religious, employed with regular income, and mentally and physically able to manage the "usual" tasks of everyday life. However, when some difference sets our story apart, we become marginalized and disenfranchised from the benefits offered by the dominant narrative. Many people grow up marginalized because of skin color, sexual orientation, or disability. Others become disenfranchised from dominant narratives when people and events dramatically reinterpret or redirect their story. To survive, marginalized people and families often forcibly "bend" their own experience to fit expectations of the dominant, normative cultural narrative. Like Ralph Ellison's invisible man or Franz Kafka's prisoner, when survival demands that our own story be subjugated to socially privileged stories, humanity is sacrificed to various forms of madness.

What does this have to do with pastoral care when a person tries to take his or her own life? First, suicide attempts often signal the fact that important personal or community stories have been subjugated and are in need of liberating care.[4] For instance, a sexually abused teen may become suicidal trying to subjugate her story to community expectations of nonabusive families. Second, a suicide attempt—particularly a first attempt—dramatically alters personal and community meanings. They turn stories inside out and present a difference that disenfranchises an individual and family from the central cultural narrative. After surviving an overdose, one teen described this as a "stigma." She had been the "smart one" headed for the best colleges—until she returned to school and was surrounded by others' knowledge of her attempt. In any attempted suicide, social equity is lost; the family no longer matches expectations. A person who fails in a suicide attempt is reclassified as a "suicide risk," "manipulative," or "mentally ill." Others do not recognize the experience and do not know how to respond apart from directing such odd experience back toward guiding cultural norms.

When a parishioner has attempted suicide, pastors are confronted with individuals and families whose stories no longer make sense. Often, they are trapped in a cloud of secrecy, shame, and confusion. Pastors are in a unique position to hear these painful and disorienting stories of a person's decision to end life. These stories are complex and filled with nuances of a suicidal person's relationship with self, family, church, community, and God. This means that pastors must be exceptional story hearers. Care must begin with sensitivity to how an attempt survivor's story intersects (or fails to intersect) with dominant cultural and religious narratives. Transformation, the hope of all liberative care, depends on hearing people well enough to help them find a better voice for their experience than suicide. This kind of hearing requires safe physical and psychological space for deeply meaningful life-and-death stories to emerge. Physical space must guarantee confidentiality and an invitation to disclose. Conversations should take place in a comfortable office or home with a guarantee of no interruptions.

Psychological space requires preparation by a pastoral listener. Listening well requires making peace with "losing" time that could be used for other pastoral priorities. It means releasing personal ruminations in order give full honor to a story loaded with anxiety and potential rejection. Creating psychological space may also mean suspending previous judgment contained in professional narratives describing the family's experience. By definition, these narratives are privileged. They exert power and subjugate important personal and family stories. Suspending previous judgment does not mean these interpretations are dismissed as irrelevant. In fact, they often contain important information to help protect potentially suicidal people or facilitate transformation. However, they must not overshadow individual, family, or religious self-understanding. Liberative care starts from a "not knowing" position that hears individual and family stories through ears unhindered by certainty ascribed by dominant professional narratives. Stories of attempted suicide are valid in their own right. They draw us into genuine experience of the "other." They place pastoral hearers in a privileged position to discover with a family a new interpretation of God's radically inclusive love or refreshed visions of participation in the community of Christ.

Praxis—that back and forth motion between action and reflection characteristic of liberation methods—is set in motion by hearing stories through new ears and seeing concrete, particular events through the eyes of those who suffer. Robert McAfee Brown[5] outlines five points for effective praxis:

- Praxis avoids abstractions. It is related to specific situations of real people in everyday life;
- Action-reflection related to these specific situations is always about transforming the present. Truth is something done, not discovered;
- Praxis is not about finding solutions for people; it is about empowering the oppressed to change their own situation;
- Praxis is not a solitary project. It is the activity of a community engaged in an intentional cycle of action and reflection;
- Praxis is not a tool of orthodoxy. It is a method of constructive theology that is never complete. It is always willing to be corrected by truth emerging in action.

Praxis listens to the human pain of particular suicide stories unrestrained by normative social convention or the censor of expert interpretation. It avoids professional generalizations such as "dysfunctional family" or "suicide attempter." Instead, it stays in the concrete specifics of what people feel, do, and believe. Praxis refuses to categorize one particular kind of behavior—a suicide attempt—as something strange and beyond the scope of religious care within the community of faith. Instead, it is a method to examine from within the community of faith those elements of social or physical life that create and support suffering. Praxis is not a form of therapy to change suffering, suicidal people to fit their circumstances better. It is a model of transformation that intends to change both those who suffer and the social context in which they live. Mutual transformation is possible when:

- Careful listening invites subjugated stories into the life of the community;
- Those who suffer respond to the invitation;
- The community makes its resources available for the process of action-reflection and empowerment of those who suffer.

In practice this means that pastoral care begins by responding to a person or family but then quickly moves to engage the community of faith. Listening deeply to the story of a person who has attempted suicide will jar pastoral sensibilities. If we have listened well, we will be unsettled. We are likely to find that our traditional religious and moral certainties fall short when confronted by this new situation. This presses us into a constructive theological conversation with the Christian community and our theological sources. At this point we become full companions with those receiving care. Central questions such as, "Where is God when life hurts so much I want to kill myself?" or "How can I live when it feels like there is no reason to live?" or "How do I repair relationships disrupted by trying to kill myself?" are shared fully by the pastor and the community of faith. Instead of offering easy answers based on dominant narratives, liberative praxis leads the community of faith into a creative, reflective process that empowers those needing care to find transforming answers. In this process, all participants are transformed. "Hermeneutical circulation"—the basic motion of liberative praxis—describes how story-transforming reflection can take place in the Christian community.[6] (Fig. 2)

The following case study illustrates how liberative praxis moving through hermeneutical circulation can guide pastoral care and transformation.

Irene J.

Irene was a twenty-five-year-old mother of two young children (two-year-old James and five-year-old Rachel). She and Rob married after high school and moved from their childhood

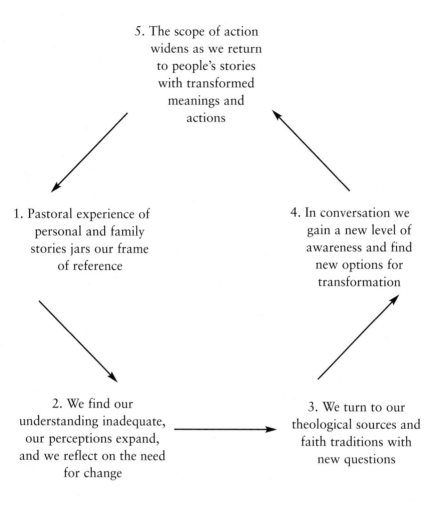

5. The scope of action widens as we return to people's stories with transformed meanings and actions

1. Pastoral experience of personal and family stories jars our frame of reference

4. In conversation we gain a new level of awareness and find new options for transformation

2. We find our understanding inadequate, our perceptions expand, and we reflect on the need for change

3. We turn to our theological sources and faith traditions with new questions

Figure 2

home to a nearby city. Rob found a job working for a national delivery service. Irene's plan to become a travel agent was "put on hold" for her first pregnancy. As Rob's job became more demanding, Irene became a permanent stay-at-home mom. Though finances were never good for the couple, their problems were compounded when James was born prematurely with serious health problems. In the two years since James's birth, Rob has worked overtime and at weekend jobs to meet financial obligations. Prior to James's birth, the couple had attended church regularly and had developed a circle of friends. However, with little money or time, the couple soon grew socially isolated. Work and James's health demands rarely allowed the couple to attend church or participate in group activities.

Over a two-year period, conflict escalated between Irene and Rob, centered on Rob's frequent absences and his minimal responsibility for the children. The morning after a particularly intense fight, Irene drove forty miles to her parents' house. She asked her mother to watch the children while she returned home to take care of things she could not do while watching two children. Irene returned home, drank half a bottle of bourbon, and ingested the contents of all the prescription medications in her bathroom. When she failed to answer her cell phone, her mother called Rob. Later, emergency room physicians explained to Rob that, even in combination with alcohol, medications available to Irene would not have been fatal. She would experience some toxic effects for several days without permanent damage. A consulting psychiatrist recommended careful evaluation but doubted Irene really intended to kill herself. He suggested that Irene knew Rob would return home in a few hours, or her mother would become worried when she did not return on time. Rescue was likely in the way she designed her attempt. The psychiatrist explained that a nonfatal overdose, especially in younger women, is most often related to family conflict or relationship problems. Many women use a "suicide gesture" to attract attention, manipulate an intimate relationship, or punish important people in their lives. Her attempt was not serious enough to warrant hospital admission, which would add financial stress to the couple's problems. Instead, outpatient therapy was recommended to assess the potential for a "repeat performance," to treat personality problems driving Irene's suicidal behavior, and to intervene with relational problems related to her attempt.

Irene was unwilling to speak of her attempt other than to reassure Rob and her parents that she was no longer thinking of harming herself. She did not want her children to suffer. When Rob pressed her about why she wanted to die, Irene said only that "the stress just got too much. I just kind of got overwhelmed, but it's better now." One week later, Rob became angry with Irene's unwillingness to talk about her attempt and told her that trying to punish him with a suicide attempt wasn't fair. Irene exploded—Rob didn't know what he was talking about. She was trying to punish no one. Her life was too hard. She couldn't manage the stress, and death had seemed like the best option. How dare he be so selfish and think this was all about him? He wasn't around enough to understand the kind of pressure she lived with. He certainly would never understand the humiliation and self-loathing she felt because of her unsuccessful attempt. Feeling helpless, Rob suggested that they talk with their pastor the next day. Irene agreed, though she dreaded confessing her attempted suicide.

Irene and Rob met with Pastor Blanchard in her office the day after their argument. Rob explained that he was very anxious about Irene's suicide attempt. He wanted the name of a counselor who could help her recover and guarantee that she would not try to harm herself again. Irene did not want to see a counselor. "How will the world be better if I see someone who can tell me that what I did was wrong and that I'm screwing up my whole family's life? I know that! I'm being pressured into making everybody else feel better! I know the doctor told you I was trying to manipulate everybody with a 'suicide gesture.' How will it help to pay money we don't have to hear that again? I feel guilty enough." Pastor Blanchard responded by suggesting that the decision to see a counselor could be "put on hold" for the moment. It might be helpful if Irene could tell her own story of how she got into a position where taking her own life seemed like her only option. She asked Rob to listen with her; at some point she would also ask him about his experience.

For forty minutes Irene described how her life had become increasingly narrow and isolated. She felt intensely guilty about her feelings. She had no right to resent the fact that her own career had been stillborn. That was no one's fault, and she loved her children. How could she hold her disappointment against Rob and the kids? Financial problems and James's health made matters worse. Rob worked all the time. She was angry about having so little help managing a chronically ill child. By asking clarifying questions and probing for feelings, Pastor Blanchard helped Irene articulate the depth of isolation, pain, and anger that had permeated her life for nearly two years. She helped Irene name her disappointment in God for giving her a seriously ill child and her feelings of abandonment when friends began to avoid her. Irene expressed grief about losing hope in vocation, marriage, and parenthood. She could talk to no one. Rob was always exhausted and her parents told her to "hang in there, God won't test you beyond your endurance." At the same time she felt sick and selfish because she resented Rob's life away from home. "I'm supposed to be able to sacrifice myself for my kids and my family. I've failed as a woman, a mom, and a wife." Pastor Blanchard also helped Irene express her frustration with a church that responded when James was born but that did not follow up. She knew she was "on some prayer list." This seemed little consolation when she was feeling helpless, hopeless, and worthless. All of these things, explained Irene, simply piled up until "I felt like I was disappearing. I just couldn't do another day. Dying would be such a relief. I just prayed that Rob, my kids, and my parents would understand."

Listening to Irene's story in its concrete detail jars Pastor Blanchard. (Step one of hermeneutical circulation.) Irene's story of isolation, stress, broken dreams, and failed images of femininity makes her more than a survivor of a suicide attempt or a woman trying to manipulate attention through self-harm. Given voice, her experience places her suicidal action in a larger context of religious and cultural meaning. Looking through Irene's eyes, Pastor Blanchard finds normative cultural and religious explanations inadequate. Step two of hermeneutical circulation presses her to expand her understanding of Irene's experience and to reinterpret the nature of change in this particular circumstance. In steps three and four (fig. 2), Pastor Blanchard initiates multiple conversations with several partners. Her first task is to secure a dialogical relationship with Irene and Rob. This includes a no-suicide agreement with Irene (see chapter 2) and a covenant to explore together what the gospel of Christ means specifically for Irene and Rob's circumstance. Pastor Blanchard is careful not to promise answers, but commits to a journey that seeks transformation for Irene, Rob, their family, and the congregation.

One place to begin is to explore with Irene how dominant images of family, women, and problems have participated in the situation that frames her suicide attempt. The "problem" is not located solely within her as a psychological, spiritual, or moral failure. Instead, meanings that structure Irene's cognitive, volitional, and emotional life are formed in the social context in which she lives. Narrative family therapists assume that problems are formed in social life, but become "pathological" when they are internalized as defining characteristics of individuals. For Irene, this may mean that she has internalized her inability to live up to "reasonable" expectations of marriage, motherhood, self-sacrifice, and individual responsibility for her feelings. Her life does not fit the dominant narrative, and it is her failure that makes this so. By externalizing significant parts of the problem that Irene has internalized, Pastor Blanchard can begin the process of helping Irene "re-author" her story in ways that offer hope. For instance, instead of focusing on Irene's failure to meet important expectations (an internalization), she might explore with Irene how women are set up to internalize messages that oppress. This may include direct conversation about how women are socialized for self-sacrifice and self-denial,[7] or how women are often blamed "for their unrealistic expectations or their failure to work it all out . . ."[8] Pastor Blanchard can help Irene construct a landscape of meaning that takes seriously how her own story as woman, mother, and wife is undermined by financial oppression, an unmanageable health-care system, and inadequate congregational support for families with deep, everyday needs. This set of meanings may help Irene understand how helplessness and despair gained control of her life, and death seemed the best option. Irene as a "sick person" is removed from focus. She is an overwhelmed wife and mother. She is a marginalized person who has been separated from concrete manifestations of God's grace for her particular social location. Care can now focus on supporting Irene's subjugated story of oppression and integrating her into the broader life of the community of faith. Hope resides at the point where Irene finds a connection between her story and the story of God's inclusive love embodied in the church.

Liberative care most often begins in one-to-one conversations and direct intervention. Steps three and four (fig. 2) invite new voices into conversation. Scripture and theology may provide helpful voices. For example, Irene saw herself so overwhelmed by doing what was right that death seemed the only option. This image might lead Pastor Blanchard toward the story of Elijah's flight into the desert (1 Kings 19). In this story, Elijah's diligence and faithfulness resulted in exhaustion and despair. Like Irene, he became overwhelmed by isolation and work, which he tried to resolve with death. Without food or water he walked a day into the desert and collapsed, waiting to die of exposure. While this story may help Irene find kinship with a tradition that understands despair to the point of death, Elijah's rescue also points toward possible unique outcomes for Irene, Pastor Blanchard, and the congregation. In this story, a messenger of God appeared and sustained Elijah with the basics of life—food and water—when Elijah could not care for himself. It is instructive that this was not a solitary instance. The messenger stays with Elijah beyond his immediate collapse. When he is able to rise, the messenger sits with him while he gains strength, gives him provisions for his journey, and provides guidance for his walk to Horeb.

Images from this story can fuel active-reflective care. First, it is no small point that life-sustaining help is given with no judgment about Elijah's behavior in spite of negative Hebrew attitudes about suicide. Second, the text joins basic sustenance with intensive personal engagement that leads toward reconnection with community. Pastor Blanchard and Irene may be able to use these scriptural images to organize mutual reflection on Irene's experience. Living can be named a first priority. Her mother's concern and her husband's action give her an option to continue living and illustrate God's presence. Together they can discuss what a journey toward transformation might include. Pastor Blanchard can begin the journey by first offering bread and water to Irene—such as guiding Irene and Rob toward outpatient pastoral counseling in support of her decision to live. It might also include mobilizing congregational resources to provide hands-on help with James and financial help with overwhelming expenses. At this point, Pastor Blanchard is moving into steps three and four of hermeneutical circularity (fig. 2). She is engaging the church's resources to act in concrete, nonjudgmental support of the couple's everyday needs while also initiating a conversation that defines what transformation might mean in this particular episode of care. Her action will spur broader conversation as church leaders struggle with the theological meaning and limits of offering such concrete response. At their best, these conversations will include voices from Scripture, theology, social analysis, and ethics.

Active-reflective conversations in steps three and four will necessarily include Irene and Rob. Transformation requires that they examine their own resources and their own relationship to their community of faith. Again, biblical narrative can inform the reflective process. Preparation complete, Elijah traveled forty days and nights to Mount Horeb (1 Kings 19:8-9). While the scripture tells us nothing about his journey, it is easy to imagine God's messenger walking along with Elijah as a conversation partner and caregiver. Taking our cue from his dialogue with God on Mount Horeb, we can envision Elijah rehearsing vociferous complaints about overwhelming expectations and his alienation from his religious community (vv. 1, 14). He also faced his limitations head-on—his situation was overwhelming. Jezebel's threat to have him killed was real (vv. 1-3). Regardless of his past strength, her threat coming at that particular time sent Elijah over the edge toward suicide. In the cave Elijah's limitations were reinforced. He could not protect himself from an environment that blew and shook the world around him (vv. 9-14). His pilgrimage ends in a transforming episode of action-reflection in the middle of chaos. As the world shakes and roars around him, he cries about how unfair life has been. He questions God's wisdom and presence. He tests the foundations of his faith and purpose. In this interactive process, Elijah finds God in the fact that his story/complaint is heard and taken seriously: "Elijah, why are you here?" "I am here because I've been conscientious! I've worked hard and done what was expected! I'm all alone, and I can't do it anymore!" Action-reflection resulted in community and personal transformation. Elijah was reconnected to his religious community in a new way. His eyes were opened to see others who shared his commitments and understood the task he carried (seven thousand who have not bowed to Baal, vv. 5-18). He was directed to companions who shared his work and could be a positive emotional presence in difficult times. Finally, he was reminded that his presence, life, and ministry were important.

This kind of theological reflection can help structure a context of transformation for Irene, Pastor Blanchard, and the congregation. Together they can explore a new narrative in which Irene's story intersects with religious life. This can take many forms. For instance, conversation with Pastor Blanchard may empower Irene toward engaging resources within the congregation in new ways. Her story can then become part of the discourse of the community as she engages others about help she needs with James, as she finds ways to meet her own needs in congregational relationships, or as she willingly advocates for congregational intervention for families with chronic health-care and financial problems. Her advocacy can magnify the cycle of action-reflection as the community confronts a call to action and is forced to think theologically about what this means for the community.

Irene may be unable to advocate for herself. In this case, Pastor Blanchard may need to take a more active role. She may point Irene toward a changed vision of herself in relationship with the community of faith. This might include connecting her to programs that provide home assistance or to women's groups that explore new images of femininity and motherhood less deadly to her spirit. Pastor Blanchard may need to gather selected leaders and temporarily speak for Irene by challenging congregational narratives that intersect with Irene's subjugated story. For example, she may question the church's individualistic ethos that "stays out of people's business" and takes no action when James's illness keeps Irene from choir and other supportive activities. Transformation may begin by leaders acting—perhaps by providing care for James so Irene can sing in the choir—and then reflecting on how families are unintentionally marginalized through lack of attention. As hermeneutical circulation moves from steps three and four to step five, both stories, the congregation's and Irene's, are changed.

Effective liberative praxis anchors itself in multiple sources. In Irene's case, Pastor Blanchard and congregational leaders may begin by reflecting on a biblical story that helps underscore how Irene's story meets the congregation's story. They may also be stimulated to act by other church members' stories of despair met by grace and love. As they continue the process, they may find important voices about suicide in the social sciences, or about despair and hope in the theological literature. When listening to these multiple voices, it is important for Pastor Blanchard and congregational leaders to keep reflection and action close to this specific episode of care. It is far too easy to avoid transformation with abstract knowledge. Praxis becomes alive as it informs specific acts of care in Pastor Blanchard's preaching, teaching, reorganization of congregational responses to isolated church members, and pastoral conversations with Irene and her family.

SUICIDE ATTEMPTS—MULTIPLE STORIES

Irene's story is not a paradigm of "attempted suicide." In fact, liberative praxis rejects categorical explanations as a form of oppression. The individual context of any suicide attempt will determine where reflection starts, what care is needed, and what shape transformation might take. However, social analysis and biopsychosocial study of factors that influence particular patterns of self-harm are important conversation partners. These can help describe the fabric of individual stories and inform preventive and responsive care.

An attempted suicide is a deeply emotional event for pastors, congregations, family, and the actor. It is frightening, often infuriating, behavior. Trends discovered through suicide research can help contain some of this anxiety.

Lethality after an Initial Attempt

Though any attempt to take one's life is serious and requires intervention, studies show that roughly 90 percent of all people who make an unsuccessful suicide attempt die of natural causes. Stated another way, over a thirty-five to forty-year period, only about 10 percent of persons who have made an earlier attempt will eventually kill themselves. More specifically, in the first year after an attempt, only one person in one hundred will try again successfully. This rate continues to decline with distance from the initial attempt.[9] These studies suggest that pastors can have some confidence in their part of post-attempt intervention.

CONTINUUM OF ATTEMPTED SUICIDE

Pastors can benefit by understanding the continuum of nonlethal suicidal behavior. This continuum is not well delineated by suicide experts. Each part of the range is populated by a series of subsets that make clear distinctions difficult, if not impossible. One end of the continuum represents those who report a clear intent to die using highly lethal means. Survival is highly unlikely. The second range includes ambivalence about death, less lethal action, and attempts where rescue is more likely. A third range of behavior, called indirect self-destructive behaviors, includes self-harming action that is not overt or clearly intentional. These behaviors include, for instance, alcoholism, risky and thrill-seeking behavior, some sexual disorders, eating disorders, self-mutilation, medical noncompliance, multiple surgeries, drug addiction, and some forms of accident proneness. Most self-destructive behavior (some of which may be suicidal) is partial, chronic, and long-term. Indirect self-destructive behavior may signal depression or other emotional or personality problems.

Seeing self-harm through this continuum is helpful for pastoral ministry. It allows pastors to explore individual stories knowing that not all suicide attempts are the same.

Women and Attempted Suicide

Like men, women who die through suicide are most likely to succeed with their first attempt. However, there are distinct gender differences when examining nonfatal attempts. Studies show little difference between pre-adolescent boys and girls who make suicide attempts. However, by mid-teens, girls outnumber boys in suicide attempts by at least 4 to 1[10] and possibly as high at 10 to 1.[11] One study of fifteen to twenty-four-year-old women showed two hundred suicide attempts for every completed suicide (200:1) compared with a ratio of 26:1 for men the same age.[12] Though peaking in young adulthood, this pattern remains consistent throughout the female adult lifespan and across cultures.

Women (especially younger women) are also more likely than men to make multiple attempts. Clinical observers often interpret women's attempt at self-harm as impulsive and related to changes in important social relationships and family conflict. Professional opinions often state that women's nonfatal attempts are manipulative or expressions of revenge and anger rather than intent to die. In one study, psychiatrists found that nearly 70 percent of nonfatal suicide attempts (mostly women) were intended to frighten or manipulate others without intent to die.[13] Patients in the study universally disagreed and believed that professionals were making these attributions in error.[14]

Several studies have examined women's suicide attempts in the cultural context in which they occur. These scholars suggest that women's socialization demands success in relationships. Meaning and value are related to preserving relationships, establishing networks of care, and embodying responsibility in relationships. When these relational meanings are threatened, women become vulnerable to suicide.[15] These factors help explain women's more frequent attempts at suicide, choice of less lethal means, and lower success rate than men. Women's suicide attempts often focus attention on unmet relational needs. At the same time, women are less willing to abandon important relationships through death and are more likely than men to attend to how those left behind will fare without them. This relational focus suggests that women's attempts are not expressions of dependency or relational pathology, but represent "a desperate plea for engagement under conditions of threat to that connection."[16] One study showed that employment may reduce female vulnerability to suicide by increasing opportunities for adult relationships.[17]

Suicide attempts are strongly correlated with mental disorders. In American culture, women are more likely than men to be diagnosed with depressive illness (most likely to result in suicide) and twice as likely to be prescribed mood-modifying drugs. When anorexia (often considered a form of suicide) is added to the equation, this gendered distinction becomes staggering. Pastoral theologian Christie Neuger[18] relates this to several powerful depressogenic realities for women. Patriarchal injustices assure that women have less power in cultural value, less economic independence, and more vulnerability to physical abuse. Women, suggests Neuger, are born into a culture that disadvantages them and puts them at risk for intimate violence. As girls develop surrounded by gendered norms and power arrangements, they are denied "the ability to develop a comprehensive sense of trust, industry, or identity, no matter how stable or affirming their family life or personality."[19] Consequently, women have learned to subjugate their own stories and interpret their own experiences, needs, and goals through those they have been taught to appease. They become a supporting cast with no serious voice or authority. These social realities set the context for women's self-blame as victims in abusive relationships and for self-destructive behavior in suicide attempts.

Young women grow up in a cultural world characterized by sexism, sexualization, and sexual violence. There is good evidence that as many as one in three girls is sexually assaulted by the age of eighteen. Girls are the victims of such violence about three times as often as boys. Pamela Cooper-White suggests that these facts have a serious impact on a girl's developmental process that has yet to be fully explored. "[W]e all live in a 'rape culture' in which women's and girl's experience are surrounded every day by media messages that female bodies are meant to be used as commodities, and that violations of female body-selves will be ignored, tacitly condoned, or blamed on them."[20] It is not surprising that suicide studies have found that over 30 percent of adolescents hospitalized for a suicide attempt reported a history of sexual abuse. Females in the study were significantly more likely to have been abused than males and were more likely to make suicide attempts.[21] These studies suggest that higher frequency of attempts among young women may be strongly linked to mental disorders related to trauma and sexual abuse. It is clear that sexual abuse can create conditions for future self-harm, particularly when results of trauma impact a woman's ability to sustain relational connections.

The frequency of women's attempted suicide cannot be written off as manipulation or "gesture" simply because women do not die as often. Women have been socialized into a dominant culture that silences important voices of experience, requires conformity to sexist and patriarchal expectations, and forces women to live quietly with the residuals of sexual trauma. Citing psychologist Miriam Greenspan, Neuger[22] proposes that beneath much female depression is an abiding, unconscious rage about oppression that has no legitimate outlet. High rates of women's attempted suicide may reflect a culture that systematically kills women rather than a collection of sick women unable to manage the stresses of everyday life. Suicidology is just now beginning to pay attention to how patriarchy and high levels of female self-destructive mental illness and attempted suicide are related.

A woman's attempted suicide should raise important local questions for pastors and congregations. What does it mean that in many cases women must self-destruct to be heard relationally? What might this observation say about how *our* families, *our* congregation, and *our* communities socialize girls, relate to women's relational needs, and model value and meaning for women? How might *our* religious leadership voice concern that women pay exorbitant tolls in mental health to sustain current family and relational structures or manage the weight of past sexual abuse? Is it possible for us, here in our particular location, to listen carefully to women's stories about conditions that set the stage for self-destruction? Is it possible for us, *here*, to claim a public theological voice to question how women's voices of pain are silenced by suicide stereotypes or the stigma of ascribed mental disorder?

Lifespan Consideration

Completed suicide rates increase with age, but suicide attempts are frequent at every stage of life. Successful childhood suicide (ages five to fourteen) is very rare. Though success is rare, suicidal and self-destructive behavior is not. Researchers believe that childhood suicide attempts are grossly underreported because of the stigma attached to the behavior. Children do act out on suicidal impulses, but because they often lack access to lethal means and are developmentally unable to form an effective plan, completion rates are low. Though identifying children at risk is difficult, researchers have identified patterns associated with greater risk. Like adults, depressed children are at greatest risk. Unlike adults, childhood depression is often masked and requires diagnosis by professionals trained specifically to identify childhood depression. It is not uncommon for depressed children to display behavior problems, symptoms similar to attention deficit disorder, or to express feelings of hopelessness or worthlessness to friends, teachers, and church leaders. Many depressed children are isolated and report feeling lonely for months prior to a suicide attempt. Attempts in children are frequently associated with chaotic or unpredictable circumstances over which they have no control. Parents who suffer from alcoholism, affective disorder, and marital conflict are likely to have depressed children. Chaotic parents often model ineffective and impulsive coping strategies that may relate to suicidal behavior in children.[23] Many suicidal children have had contact with a family friend or relative who has attempted or completed suicide.

Adolescent suicide attempts became a cause for concern with a dramatic "baby boomer" escalation between 1950 and 1990. This pattern may be associated with changes in adolescent expectations in post-World War II urban, industrial culture. Prior to World War II, older adolescents quickly entered adult life through marriage and vocation. Post-World War II teens were expected to delay entry into adult life. Most were isolated in school for longer periods of time and were discouraged from marrying young, thus blocking meaningful sexual and vocational experiences. Post-war prosperity added pressure to succeed in an increasingly achievement-oriented society. Some social analysts have speculated that this kind of developmental "moratorium" is related to teen countercultural behavior, crime, substance abuse, and self-destruction. In today's world, suicide is the third leading cause of death for adolescents. Teen attempted suicide is common. Like adults, adolescent girls are more at risk for attempted suicide, while boys are more likely than girls to succeed by using firearms or other violent means.

Teen suicidal behavior seems to be related to several primary factors. First, while depressive illness increases across the lifespan, the most dramatic increase takes place in children and adolescents between nine and nineteen years old. Teen depression is common and underreported. At all ages, suicidal thoughts are associated with depression. One study[24] found that 85 percent of teens diagnosed with depression reported significant suicidal thoughts. Nearly one-third of depressed teens attempted suicide before turning twenty. Second, alcohol and drug abuse rise dramatically in teen years. One clear research finding is the strength of relationship between alcohol abuse and suicidal behavior. Nearly 70 percent of teens who complete suicide have a history of alcohol abuse. About half of teens attempting suicide have a history of significant alcohol use and reported drinking shortly before their suicide attempt. Alcohol, depression, and suicidal thoughts form a deadly brew. This is particularly true for adolescents, who can be impulsive, have not developed adult coping strategies, and experience the usual lapses of judgment common to teen years.

Relational disruptions and stressful life circumstances are a third and very significant factor in teen suicide. Security and comfort in personal relationships seem to be critical for teen suicide immunity. Actual or potential loss through conflict, humiliation, or shame appears to be a primary issue. Arguments with parents, difficulties in romantic relationships, moving away from home, and legal or disciplinary problems are the most frequent precursors to an adolescent suicide attempt. Suicide potential increases when a teen also experiences emotional disturbances or psychological problems. These are not limited to depressive illnesses. About one third of boys making suicide attempts were diagnosed with aggressive and antisocial problems rather than depression.[25] Long-term, intractable family conflict may predispose some youth to suicidal behavior by undermining coping skills needed for supportive relationships.

Conflicts around emerging sexuality are common for most teens and appear to be active in most instances of attempted teen suicide. Most striking are recent studies suggesting that gay and lesbian youth are two to three times more likely than heterosexual adolescents to have suicidal thoughts and make suicide attempts.[26] However, like their heterosexual counterparts, gay and lesbian youth reported "family problems" as the primary reason for their suicide attempt and not confusion about sexual orientation or conflicts about sex.[27] This finding reinforces that effective, supportive family relationships may be the single most important prevention for suicidal behavior in youth. Helping families in conflict or crisis—particularly around youth who may be "coming out" as gay or lesbian—may be the single best pastoral care action to prevent adolescent suicide attempts.

Finally, adolescents who try to take their own lives are likely to have friends or family who have made similar attempts. One study[28] found that about 40 percent of teens completing suicide had a close relative who had previously attempted or completed suicide.

Clinical experience suggests that parents may be slow to respond to adolescents at risk. It is not unusual for parents to interpret their teens' personal, social, and relational distress as a temporary "stage" that will spontaneously disappear. Most parents do not want to believe their child is depressed or at risk. This leaves many depressed teens without treatment as parents underestimate the pain of social failure or breakup in their child's first significant sexual relationship.

Midlife (mid-thirties through fifties) presents serious developmental challenges. The same baby-boomer population that experienced a dramatic rise in adolescent/young adult suicide attempts after 1950 appeared to carry this into middle adulthood. While the rate of completed suicide for midlife adults has changed little over time, new studies show a connection between midlife attempts and adult developmental tasks. Suicide can be the ultimate sign of developmental stagnation. By the time most people reach midlife, a number of life stresses have accumulated. Careers have not gone as planned, energy for living is not what it once was, relationships have changed or ended, children have left home, and loved ones are lost to death. Negotiation of midlife requires coping with loss and change. Earlier coping strategies may be stretched beyond their limits by normal midlife, or a number of rapid changes may overwhelm previously effective strategies.

[S]ome midlifers simply cannot negotiate the midlife transition. For example, they can no longer take pleasure in their work and cannot give up the illusions and tyranny of youth—especially if they have nagging, chronic physical illnesses;

recurring depressive disorders; alcohol problems and low economic, emotional, and spiritual resources. Midlife often means (as Hemingway and Styron found out) that one must continue to live without the help of alcohol, work advances, or sexual acting out. Some midlife men kill themselves in part because they do not believe it is possible to change their young adult lifestyles and become viable middle-age people: their "middlescence" does them in.[29]

Suicide marks failure to reevaluate life dreams and understand that happiness is elusive.

The highest rates of completed suicide are among the elderly (sixty-five and older), dominated primarily by aging white men. There are few studies examining nonfatal attempts in the aging population, partly because those who attempt suicide are highly successful with their first attempt. Recent opinion polls suggest that most elderly people in the United States find good reasons for continuing life. In fact, while the oldest part of the population has expanded over the past decade, the suicide rate for those over sixty-five has slightly decreased. Older people are finding ways to remain productive and active in life. Nevertheless, a significant minority experience overwhelming personal losses of important relationships, independence, social support, health, and finances. These losses, coupled with lifelong personality or mental health problems, appear to tax coping strategies beyond their limits. It is particularly important for pastors to understand that the suicide rate for white males over age eighty-five is three times higher than that for younger people. Researchers suggest that these men are more likely than others to refuse to accept declining physical health, are less adaptable to multiple life changes, and tend toward rigid patterns of thinking. These characteristics increase their vulnerability to suicide. One leading suicidologist[30] has suggested that elderly suicide has much to do with an inability (or refusal) to accept the terms of the human condition. Age appears to have an opposite effect for white women and African

American men and women. The rate of attempted and completed suicide drops significantly for these people in old age, perhaps partly because earlier life experience has taught them to adapt in ways not required of white men.

Special Cases

There is no simple suicide attempt. However, attempts can be more or less complex. Sometimes responding to an attempt is straightforward. Other times an attempt will embody a rich texture of hopelessness that defies intervention. Suicidal behavior is often associated with multiple stressors and serious mental health problems. When these factors coalesce with chronic problems in living, systems of care can be overwhelmed. In such cases, a pastor's intervention skills may be seriously challenged, and a congregation may be pressed to the extreme limits of their ability to embody God's inclusive love. At the same time, congregational care may be the only consistent help available for suicidal individuals with multiple problems and little social equity.

Mary

Mary is forty-five years old, has never been married, and lives alone with her three dogs. Three years ago a parishioner referred Mary to Pastor Gray for help with rent and grocery money. Mary was unemployed and had recently been hospitalized overnight when paramedics responded to an apparent suicide attempt reported by a neighbor. She began attending services and eventually found a part-time job with the help of parishioners. Over time Mary has stayed on the periphery of congregational activities. Church members tell Pastor Gray it is difficult to relate to her. She appears to have few friends and finds most of her companionship with her dogs. Mary has regularly called Pastor Gray in crisis over the past two years. During these episodes Mary is overwhelmed by intense feelings, problems in living, and perceived relational slights by coworkers and church members. These are often expressed in rage and helplessness that seem out of proportion to the situation.

Pastor Gray has grown frustrated with Mary's frequent and time-consuming problems and her pervasive allusions to suicide as a way out of her pain. His initial attempt to refer Mary for professional counseling was fruitless. Mary had exhausted resources available to her in the local mental health system. She had a history of repeated psychiatric hospitalization with a diagnosis of borderline personality and bipolar disorder. Her therapist, whom Pastor Gray consulted with Mary's permission, explained that Mary was seen once a month to monitor her medication. He considered her chronically mentally ill and offered little hope for improvement. She was unlikely to be hospitalized again unless a serious, life-threatening suicide attempt demanded medical intervention.

During pastoral conversations, Pastor Gray discovered that Mary had a long history of suicide attempts. Mary reported that she was an incest survivor, and suicide "lived inside" her. It was a constant companion. It was her way out of pain that never goes away. On good days it stayed in the back of her mind as a safety net. On bad days it was an active presence—every minute was a battle between continuing to live in pain or retreat to the security of death.

After two years of care with Mary, Pastor Gray feels hopeless. None of his responses seem to have any lasting effect. He is tired of fielding complaints from parishioners about Mary's "negative influence" on the congregation. He has grown resentful of the time and anxiety involved in responding to Mary's suicide-laden crisis calls. So far, Mary's no-suicide contract has worked. Pastoral conversations seem to keep her from killing herself, though there is no notable improvement in her overall functioning. Pastor Gray is angry that there are so few resources for Mary and that so much responsibility falls to him. He wonders if his continued availability is undermining other parts of his ministry and whether Mary's helplessness is worsened by his agreement to be so available to her. He is tempted to turn the problem over to someone else by immediately notifying Emergency Medical Services the next time Mary calls with suicidal intent. However, he knows from Mary's experience and consultation with her therapist that this will accomplish little. Without life-threatening injuries, Mary will not be hospitalized or receive substantial help. It is likely that Mary will experience a call to EMS as a betrayal that will end her relationship with Pastor Gray and the congregation.

Mary's case is not rare. Chronically mentally ill people who are poorly served by inadequate mental health systems often turn to the church. Many of these people have suicide histories. For the most part, pastors and parishioners do not knowingly invite Mary or her deep needs into congregational life. Few pastors are trained to manage care of chronically ill, suicidal people. Few congregations would interpret their primary mission as caring for people with such deep needs. Most would prefer that Mary find her support in other community programs. Nevertheless, "Marys" show up unannounced at congregational doors. She (or he) may appear with simple needs, attracted by the compassion of well-meaning people. Parishioners who respond often underestimate the emotional cost in compassion fatigue and secondary trauma of living so close to Mary's pain. Pastors quickly discover they are trapped between very real limits of their training, time, and congregational priorities and turning away very wounded people. This is an unpleasant dilemma not easily resolved. Trading Mary's care for other pastoral priorities can leave Mary bereft; pastor and parishioners inherit a troubling ambivalence of guilt and relief.

There is no formula for Mary's care. However, her experience and Pastor Gray's frustration can stimulate liberative praxis similar to that illustrated by Irene's case. Hearing Mary's story over time can jar Pastor Gray into questioning what Mary's appearance means to him and to the congregation's Christian self-identity. How does ministry take place with such difficult people? Broadening the scope of action and reflection can spark creativity and expand options that ease Pastor Gray's individual burden with Mary. Never-imagined resources from the congregation may emerge. For instance, church members may explore their own calling to become trained in suicide intervention. Congregational leaders may decide to join the local mental health association and lobby forcefully for expanded programming to help Mary and others like her. Vocal advocates, motivated by personal contact with Mary's story, may successfully demand new space in tightly controlled mental health programs to accommodate some of Mary's more pressing needs. The congregation's spiritual development also may be enhanced by reflecting deeply on biblical narratives that recall how God's redemptive action may come unexpectedly through marginalized people who can find no room in the inn.

At some time during their ministry, most pastors will respond to a person or family who has survived a suicide attempt. These episodes of care, while frightening, offer an almost unparalleled opportunity for transformation. Important issues of personal meaning, life and death, and self-in-relationship are held in bold relief to a near-death experience. Referral to a qualified counselor or mental health professional is right and necessary. At the same time, pastors and religious leaders must not abdicate responsibility for religious care and the theological conversations that transform personal and congregational narratives. Careful pastoral listening to the storied context of a suicide attempt can open a new world of intervention when guided by liberative praxis. These processes can be transforming for the one making a suicide attempt, for families, and for congregations.

3

Suicide Vulnerability and Life in Christian Community

Pastoral care for depressed and suicidal people is most often thought of as direct counseling or crisis intervention. However, pastoral care is also expressed in preaching and teaching and how congregational life is organized. All of these impact how people interpret God's love, how individuals organize their personal spiritual journey, and how a congregation responds to people in need. A congregation's ethos, pattern of beliefs, and expectations of members will influence lifestyle choices, attitudes toward developmental changes, and strategies for coping with stress. Together, these can be powerful factors in how people manage depression and how suicide is interpreted as an option.

Though there is little research about how religion and suicide interact, there is modest evidence that religious life provides some protection against suicide.* Statistically, people who attempt or complete suicide are less likely to attend church than those who do not. The group most likely to die of suicide—Protestant males—has the lowest rate of church attendance. Those least likely to die—African American

---

*Apocalyptic cults, such as People's Temple (Jonestown), Heaven's Gate, or Branch Davidians would be exceptions. Religious groups that incorporate suicide into their values or prepare for the end days through suicide dramatically escalate risk. Usually, these suicides are the decision of the cult leader.

women—have the highest rate of church attendance. This, of course, is very thin evidence. Studies over the past twenty years have provided some information about how and what kinds of religious life buffer depression and suicide. In this chapter, I will highlight some important findings and briefly explore their meaning for congregational life.

RELIGIOUS LIFE AND MENTAL HEALTH

Over the past half-century, research has shown clear connections between biochemistry and mood and between religious experience and our biochemistry.

A number of studies confirm that religious practice* has a measurable and generally positive impact on physical, mental, and emotional well-being.[1] It is more difficult to describe exactly *what* religious behaviors, beliefs, or practices produce this positive impact, or exactly *how* religion acts to buffer stress or improve coping. Researchers have explained positive effects in several ways. One position asserts that religion is a condition of human life and is fundamentally beneficial. Some neuroscientists now argue that the human brain itself is "religiogenetic."[2] They argue that our human brain is structured in a way that makes us fundamentally religious. This accounts for the fact that religious expression is universal across human cultures. Furthermore, religious sentiment and behavior is grounded in the same brain and neural processes that also ground psychological experience and behavior. Human wellness relies (at least partly) on actualizing religious dimensions of human experience. People with clear religious commitments and regular religious behavior are grounded in their biochemical and emotional humanity

---

* Religion in its broadest sense includes (1) belief in God or other spiritual presence or moral ideal that frames human life, (2) individual and communal ritual or celebration in some form, (3) a system of morality, and (4) a community of shared belief.

in a way that protects them from serious psychological problems when stress occurs.

A second position suggests that at the extremes of human life (such as deep bereavement, serious mood disorder, or disability), people intrinsically become more religious. Religion in these cases acts as a palliative to reduced suffering and contributes a sense of control. A third position proposes that religion is a social preventative—it preempts behaviors and attitudes that cause problems, such as unsafe sex, divorce, and alcohol consumption. Finally, a number of researchers suggest that religion is embedded in how humans survive and thrive as social creatures. In times of crises, stress, or illness, religion provides a network effect that mobilizes social resources for people in distress. These positions agree on one common factor: religion and spirituality are important factors for people managing the biological and social consequences of stress and mental illness.

DEPRESSION AND SUICIDE

There is good evidence that religious life provides protection specifically for depression and suicide. As early as 1897, sociologist Émile Durkheim noted that people who integrated religion into the whole of their life had a lower risk of suicide.[3] A number of studies since 1970 refined this observation by asking the question, "What kind of religion provides protection from depression and suicide?" Psychologist Gordon Allport[4] distinguished "intrinsic" from "extrinsic" religious motivation. Intrinsically motivated people move toward religion as an end in itself. Religion is the foundation for life meaning and important life decisions. Extrinsic motivation, however, is more utilitarian. Extrinsically motivated people may temporarily "find religion" to help in a time of crisis or participate in religious community because of its secondary benefits (such as improving business contacts or pleasing a spouse). It fluctuates with changing life situations, peer pressure, and personal need. Studies using this distinction show that persons with an intrinsic religious orientation report less depression than extrinsically religious people across all denominational boundaries.[5] Several recent studies suggest that "internalized" religion is associated with positive mental health benefits. People who see their personal faith as an organizing principle of life are less anxious, feel less guilty, and worry less than those who are extrinsically motivated.[6] Individuals who integrate personal devotion into their daily life and emphasize the centrality of their relationship with God are less depressed.[7] High intrinsic religiosity appears also to speed recovery from depression.[8] One study concluded that participation in institutional religion *without* personal devotion actually increases psychological distress.[9]

Because suicide rates are low and church attendance rate is high among African Americans,* several studies have examined the protective role of religion in African American communities. Findings generally confirmed that African Americans were similar to Euro Americans in one respect. Those who related life satisfaction to their relationship with God and saw religious life as a way to cope with challenges were less likely to consider suicide an acceptable option.[10] However, these studies revealed several distinctions. First, compared to Euro Americans, African Americans' religious community tended to extend beyond church walls and act as an integrating factor for the whole of social life. Church membership was not isolated to certain times and locations but was a basic organizing principle of the individual and family's social connections, activities, and decisions. This strong "network effect" alone appeared to be a protective factor against suicide.

Second, African American churches appeared to have a less ambivalent attitude toward suicide. This included:

---

* These factors may not account for young African American men who attend church less often than their older counterparts and are the most likely in American culture to die violently. Researchers speculate that violent death in these men may be a form of suicide.

(1) Specific teaching that suicide was not an acceptable means to solve life problems; (2) messages that suicide was the "unforgivable sin," and (3) an ethos that suicide was antithetical to being African American—it was a "White thing."[11] Finally, depressed African Americans were more likely (in one study, three times more likely) than Euro Americans[12] to see a connection between spirituality and depression and seek religious intervention. Empirical observations further substantiated that African Americans most likely to attempt suicide were young, usually homeless, and had no religious affiliation.[13]

Research suggests that people for whom religious life is personally and socially important are less likely to consider suicide a viable option. The *kind* of religious experience in the worshiping community also appears to be a protective factor. Suicide rates appear to be lower among people

- who attend churches with a congregational polity and so are more included in religious decision-making and leadership;
- who attend churches with more conservative theologies that take specific stands against suicide;
- who attend churches that maintain a high tension between their teaching and the larger culture.

Other protective factors may be found in how religious involvement interacts with coping strategies for life stress.

COPING WITH LIFE STRESSORS

Large-scale opinion polls show that most Americans (50 to 80 percent) believe that religion is helpful when facing a major life crisis or loss. Controlled studies were more modest, suggesting that religion (long-standing religious beliefs, congregational attendance, faith in God, and a set of religious ideals) was important at least half the time in coping with loss of a spouse, debilitating disease, depression, disability, or other severe crises. This is not an insignificant finding. By comparison, it is a rare drug approved by the FDA that demonstrates positive effects in half of all cases studied. Statistical significance relies on far smaller differences. Though outcomes vary dramatically from study to study, there is good evidence that religious life facilitates positive coping *for people who claim religion as an important value in all of their life.* These positive benefits do not appear to be present for people who do not see themselves as religious. One particularly helpful analysis (reviewed below) suggests that religious coping can be helpful, harmful, or mixed. This is largely dependent upon the nature of the community in which religious life is lived and the person's belief system. Results of these studies have important pastoral implications for suicide prevention and for responding to survivors when suicide is completed.

Helpful Religious Coping

Pergament and Brant's[14] review of forty studies suggests that there are three forms of helpful religious coping—positive spiritual support, congregational support, and benevolent religious reframing. ***Positive spiritual support*** appears when individuals see their relationship with God as a collaboration or partnership. This is often concrete and personal. God is physically and emotionally present. God is reassuring ("God will take care of me"). God gives personal and direct guidance about what to do or how to respond. These responses are associated with higher levels of psychological adjustment to a variety of stressors. ***Congregational support*** is bi-directional and includes both clergy and congregation. Positive coping is promoted when a person in crisis experiences freedom to ask for support from his or her pastor or congregation and when pastor or congregation offers support spontaneously. Support includes basic physical sustenance, emotional support, and help with problem solving.

Benevolent religious reframing interprets negative events as contained in the care of a loving God. Uncontrollable negative events are not random or a form of punishment. Instead, God is in control of history. Suffering may not be understandable to the human mind, but God will transform pain and make it meaningful in some way. Statements like "my pain is part of God's will" or "God has a purpose in my suffering" are not the best-formed theological statements. However, they do point to the fact that people who find redemptive religious meaning in their physical and psychological pain recover more quickly and are better protected from suicidal despair than those who cannot find such meaning. The more control of temporally uncontrollable events (illness, etc.) individuals attributed to God, the better individuals adjusted to stress. One pastoral task is to help people articulate "God is in control of what is out of my hands" in theologically beneficial ways.

Harmful Religious Coping

Religious resources can be a negative factor in coping with stress. One of the strongest findings was that a *poor or troubled relationship with one's pastor or congregation* correlates significantly with lower ability to cope with life stressors. Of course, another factor may be at work: those people who do not cope well with stress may be more likely also to have problems with their pastor or congregation. At this time studies are not sophisticated enough to evaluate this confounding variable. It is enough to note that a poor congregational relationship may decrease an individual's ability to recover from psychological and physical problems.

Negative religious reframing is also a harmful element for those trying to cope with life stress. People who reframe personal crises—or have crises interpreted by their pastor or congregation—as God's punishment are more likely to experience deep psychological distress and become worse as a result of religious intervention.

Researchers suggest that reframing stressful life events as God's punishment is not common. However, when it does occur, it has a high cost in guilt, fear, and poor recovery from physical and psychological distress. It is particularly important for pastors to attend to potential negative religious factors when religious people are faced with socially (or religiously) ambiguous stressors, such as AIDS, loss of an infant child, gay or lesbian coming out, suicide attempts, or completed suicide within a family.

Religious Coping with Mixed Results

Two forms of religious coping had mixed results. Surprisingly, use of **religious rituals** produced an ambiguous outcome. Rituals, such as confession, healing services, and mourning rites had a positive effect less than half the time and a negative effect in almost 25 percent of the cases studied. It is hard to assess what is cause and effect. Do rituals cause poorer coping or are results skewed because people with preexisting mental health problems are more likely to participate in ritual? Overall, studies suggest that it is impossible to predict what rituals, under what circumstances, and with what people will produce help, harm, or have no effect at all. These results suggest that religious leaders should use ritual only in carefully considered ways and in a context where negative outcomes can be monitored.

Coping strategies that include a partnership or collaboration with God produced mostly positive results, while **self-directing and pleading** approaches had very mixed results. Religious orientations that emphasized self-direction and personal responsibility in problem solving (God gives people freedom to direct their own lives) were related to higher levels of psychological competence. This orientation was useful when problems were indeed under human control but had negative outcomes when an individual had little real control over health or circumstances. Conversely, a deferring approach that saw God as responsible and waited for God's active intervention (such as pleading for a miracle) was related to lower levels of psychological competence. These strategies generally had negative results when problems were controllable. However, in situations beyond human influence, pleading with God appeared to provide a beneficial sense of hope and vicarious control.

IMPLICATIONS FOR PASTORAL CARE

These research findings hold few surprises for religious leaders:

- Religion is central to human existence and interacts with human embodiment in important and interesting ways.
- Religious practice and commitment has a positive impact on human psychology and biochemistry.
- People who carry deeply held religious beliefs into daily life have lower levels of depression and recover better from mood disturbances and life stressors.
- Active participation in a community of faith helps protect people from mental health problems and suicide.
- How and what churches teach about coping, depression, and suicide has an effect on how people recover from major life stressors and how suicide is interpreted as a solution to life problems.

These results highlight that pastoral care must involve more than short-term responses to people in crisis. Care is integrally related to the whole of pastoral ministry. Many of the protective factors identified in research have little to do with the counseling or crisis intervention skills of a pastor. They are related instead to discipleship, congregational life, and preaching and teaching.

Discipleship

Personal piety emerges as a very important protective factor. Pastoral counseling and crisis intervention skills are indispensable when responding to people in need. However, when counseling-based skills are overemphasized, care as spiritual leadership that enhances protective intrinsic spirituality may be overlooked. Effective care must guide parishioners toward authentic engagement with the holy that naturally intersects with daily emotional experiences, human embodiment, and social life.

Discipleship is a central concern of most Christian churches and varies widely according to tradition. Its particular "shape" (for instance, priest-led spiritual direction or evangelical Bible study groups) appears less important for wellness than the fact that individuals are developing an integrated, internalized spirituality. Faith development studies show us that deeply held, mature, and integrated personal faith creates a frame to understand and manage life's uncertainty and fragility. Pastoral care as discipleship guides people toward this mature, healthy spirituality that deepens the life of faith and organizes daily decision-making and behavior.

In his classic text, *When Religion Gets Sick*,[15] Wayne Oates notes that healthy religion is dynamic. It becomes a comprehensive philosophy of life characterized by self-examination and acceptance of human limits of power, time, and place. It provides a framework of moral consequences and is grounded in communal tradition. According to Oates, when religion gets sick, it massively hinders the basic functions of life. Instead of promoting health, religion becomes a tool to reject our basic human condition. Unhealthy religion turns toward idiosyncratic manipulation of religious symbols: If I perform the right ritual, I can make my suffering go away; or I am Christ on the cross and my suicide/death will benefit others. Sick religion tries to control an uncontrollable world through "superstition and magic [that] works to control and obliterate the unknown and the risky by the legalisms, the taboos, the rituals of incantation, and the obsessive acts that are developed as magical controls . . . Religion becomes sick when a person loads the whole responsibility for these 'thrown situations' entirely upon God and thereby thrusts the whole responsibility for changing the situation upon [God]."[16] Sick religion rejects or fragments communities of belief that could otherwise provide a protective network of support. Persons at risk for suicide are often enveloped by religious malfunction.

Discipleship toward healthy religion is an important function of pastoral care, especially as it guides an individual toward accepting both the strengths of human creation and the limitations of one's created identity in relationship to God. This allows positive collaborative possibilities: I am human and responsible for acting competently and morally in my own and others' behalf. However, I am human and there are limits. Beyond my limits there is God, upon whose ever-present and eternal care I must ultimately depend.

Of course, the challenge for all congregational leaders is to find creative ways to invite parishioners into programs, activities, and relationships that enhance ongoing, vital, and authentic personal piety. In the best of worlds, those at risk for mood disorders and suicide can be involved in discipleship prior to periods of crisis. In reality, care is often responsive to felt need. It is then necessary to find ways to invite troubled individuals into a process of spiritual growth. This may require active initiative toward people at risk for depression or other problems in living. For some parishioners, an invitation to pray together regularly, a weekly small group Bible study, or a meeting periodically to talk about one's relationship with God will be better accepted than an offer of short-term counseling or other therapy-styled intervention. This will not only provide spiritual support but also will begin a process of personal integration that relieves suffering, promotes healing, and protects against future stressors.

Raymond

Raymond was sixty-eight years old and retired when his wife died of cancer. He was a "fairly regular" member of a midsized Methodist church. He attended church once or twice per month and had never been highly engaged in church activities. Nine months after his wife's death, concerned church members reported to Pastor Avery that Raymond had lost weight, was not bathing, and rarely ventured from his house. One friend recalled that he spoke frequently of joining his wife soon. Pastor Avery had provided crisis care when Raymond's wife, Marie, had died. However, Raymond deflected interventions that seemed to him like "counseling" and refused referral to a pastoral counselor.

Responding to concern, Pastor Avery scheduled to meet Raymond at home. During the visit, he and Raymond revisited his relationship with Marie. Avoiding responses that might feel like "counseling," Pastor Avery talked with Raymond about his relationship with God and his understanding of Marie's death and his own relationship with life. The two discussed God's place in his loss and explored what kind of "claim" God had on his life as someone left behind. Confessing anger and confusion, Raymond agreed to pray with Pastor Avery every day for the next two weeks about this matter. They would meet every other day and discuss what each was discovering in prayer. The two agreed that Raymond's task in losing Marie was to find out what—if anything—God now had in store for him as the one who survived.

Over a period of two weeks, Raymond's prayers expressed anger, sadness, longing, and confusion about his own survival. Pastor Avery provided a religious sounding board. He actively reflected on scripture texts and led Raymond to discuss what "resurrection" meant for both those who die and those who are left to live with loss. At the end of two weeks Raymond accepted an invitation to meet weekly for breakfast with a group of retired men who wanted to explore ways to grow spiritually. Six months later, Raymond had faithfully attended weekly breakfasts. He actively shared in reading a spiritual growth text and reported that he was finding some meaning in surviving Marie. Though Raymond never admitted suicidal thoughts, Pastor Avery observed that he was more socially engaged, was eating regularly, and no longer made comments that implied suicide. He continued to assert that he did not believe in counseling.

Congregational Life

Relationship with a community of faith is a second, equally important protective factor. Facilitating a context for good congregational relationships is pastoral care. People who have positive congregational relationships cope better with life stressors and are less likely to take their own lives; poor congregational relationships do not protect against stressors and diminish coping skills. Practically, this means paying careful attention to how people integrate socially into congregational life, with special attention to those who appear marginalized. It is likely that people who most need the protective qualities of the church "network effect" are those who will have the most difficulty finding a place in the social life of the church. Pastors and congregational leaders may need an extra portion of creativity to find ways to engage depressed people or those who feel overwhelmed by life. These individuals rarely gravitate naturally toward relationships that will sustain them. However, pastoral initiative through repeated invitations, coordination of interactions with significant church leaders, or the attention of a well-trained care group may soften barriers to inclusion.

African American churches form a particularly strong protective "network effect" as evidenced by very low suicide rates. Many people who are at risk for depression and suicide are what pastoral theologian Edward Wimberly calls relational refugees.[17] These are people lacking nurturing and liberating relationships. They are cut off from family, community, and past generations. They lack significant connections with others to promote self-care and self-development, opting instead for destructive patterns and relationships. Wimberly asserts that African American churches house an indigenous model of mentoring that is particularly healing for relational refugees.

> African Americans employ mentoring relationships to transmit a variety of skills and to help people develop into mature and productive members of the community. Mentoring is, in fact, a model for transmitting life skills and can serve as a basis for theological education and pastoral care ministries. In situations that involve relational refugees, the mentoring model is especially helpful. Mentors can serve relational refugees as a bridge back into community, a means to overcome their feelings of homelessness. Mentors help relational refugees cultivate a worldview that orients them in terms of their self-identity, their membership in community, and their place in the world.[18]

Wimberly suggests that mentoring provides significant protection for members of African American churches. It can be equally effective in most congregations and may be one of the best ways to minister to at-risk people.

African American women, who have the lowest rates of suicide among all groups, require special attention. Factors appear to be at work that cannot be explained by either the network effect or mentoring. Womanist theologian Elaine Brown Crawford[19] observes that African American women must overcome a unique legacy of abuse and oppression. These women's suffering is contained in the particularity of black suffering. This experience is not equitable or shared equally across humanity. Black suffering is disproportionate. It is enormous in its severity. It is life-threatening and life-reducing. It is also noncatastrophic—it does not strike suddenly and leave quickly. Instead, it is transgenerational and culturally pervasive. African American women occupy a position at the depths of this suffering. They have experienced additional oppression of their bodies because of gender injustice. They have been America's "permissible victims" who could be abused with few repercussions. Crawford says, "Their existence has been scarred by the brutality and sexual exploitation of the middle passage and chattel slavery, as well as by the pervasive institutional and social forms of race, class, and gender oppression that persist to this day."[20] Nevertheless, these women seem to survive the most deadly of social contexts with the lowest rate of suicide.

Crawford suggests that African American women form a multigenerational spiritual bridge that symbolizes "our resolute refusal to die as victims, and our undaunted determination to live as vessels of hope."[21] This hope is grounded in the piercing, primal cry (or Holler) of pain, abuse, violence, and separation that connects African American women with their African ancestors. The Holler demands recognition of humanity. It marks refusal to be silenced in a world that denies their existence as women. It cries for God to "come see about me." In the midst of the Holler, African American women since the time of slavery have found hope in the shape of passion for the possible in their lives. This "unquenchable thirst for that which is not yet" provides motive for finding the audacity to live in otherwise impossible circumstances.

Through African American women's narratives, Crawford outlines an audacious hope passed from generation to generation since slavery. This hope is "a theological construct that moves these women beyond endurance to survival and, ultimately, toward the transformation of oppressive circumstances. Hope is the bridge from oppression to liberation that facilitates full humanity and fosters an undaunted passion for life."[22] This hope is eschatological, but its power is grounded in how it transforms African American women's earthly lives. Hope becomes a source of courage that makes enduring today possible and gives substance to labor for a better tomorrow. This hope provides a way for African American women to abdicate a victim role and become empowered vessels as possessors and givers of life. This hope moves women beyond the Holler and motivates them toward personal and communal potential. Hope is more than psychosocial coping. It is theological. It is rooted by faith and energized by what Crawford terms a "peculiar gospel" of resistance against oppression. Hope is anchored in the Lord Jesus with deep roots in the church, home, and community. It is not wishful thinking. It is action on behalf of themselves, their family, and their community, with the genuine expectation that hope will be fulfilled in this life and the life to come. A primary symbol for hope in the Holler is the empty cross of Christ that signals "trouble don't last always."[23]

Theologian Wendy Farley focuses on a similar sense of hope in her contemporary theodicy.[24] Christianity has struggled historically to understand how pervasive evil and suffering exist in the same world that faith insists is ordered by a gracious and powerful God. This is most clearly seen in radical suffering that cannot easily be explained by simpler concepts of humanity reaping the inevitable consequences of sin. Radical suffering is observed in victimization that destroys the human spirit and can in no way be understood as something deserved. Radical suffering is not abstract. It is concrete. It takes place in particular local situations and is experienced in personal immediacy. It is not temporary suffering or suffering necessary to achieve some goal. It is not the result of one's own action. Instead, it is undeserved and comprises a fundamental attack on a person at the very point of those things that make him or her most human. It is an assault that "pinches off" the human spirit through humiliation and pain and creates a soul incapable of self-defense. It is an incurable wound, a despair that annihilates the future, severs relationship, and empties suffering of meaning. In radical suffering "she (or he) becomes a deformed creature whose habitus is suffering. All experience is absorbed into suffering and the sufferer is impaled upon her pain. The past is gone and the future a miserable repetition of the present."[25] Clearly, Farley's vision encompasses the narratives of African American women. She explicitly includes people who are high suicide risks because of dehumanizing mental illness, physical disabilities, and trauma.

Because this suffering is not centered in one's own guilt and sin, those who experience radical suffering are beyond the reach of redemption through atonement. Instead, Farley asserts that radical suffering is relieved only through compassion. Compassion is driven by a passion for justice that not only survives tragedy but also defies it by actively refusing to the point of death to let go of human dignity. "Death may take me (or us), but I (we) will not relinquish humanity to that which oppresses." The power to resist sustains human dignity and holds the potential for meaning. Resistance takes two forms. First, conditions that cause suffering can be identified and defied through action that demands change. This is evident, for instance, in African American women's audacious survival that cares for the next generation and passes along hope that transcends multiple slaveries. Second, resistance can be deeply personal. It refuses to allow one's self or another to be degraded or treated as abnormal because of a terminal disease, chronic mental illness, or other uncontrollable circumstance. Defiance here demands dignity when utterly despairing circumstances cannot be changed. Without resistance, people can be so badly broken by pain that they participate in their own destruction.

Compassion, found in both God's willingness to "come see about me" and people who are able to enter into the experience of another's suffering, is an expression of love that undermines radical suffering and empowers defiance. It is more than an attitude or sentiment. It is effective action. Compassion requires both solidarity with suffering and opposition to its destructive effects. God is not an impotent deity who passively feels with our pain; God enters suffering with intensity and mediates action and resources necessary to overcome it. God's compassion is manifested in solidarity with suffering and defiance of all life-disrupting forms of evil. This is evident in the Exodus and coming of Christ. The Christ event holds special power: "Through interhuman compassion and justice, the reality and power of God are present to resist evil in history . . . Through compassion, creative love is augmented by the labor to restore what has been assaulted by evil and guilt. It is a work whose genius and glory are to give life and freedom to creatures who have already betrayed and been betrayed by these gifts."[26]

This is both an immediate and eschatological hope as symbolized by the Communion table to which all are invited on equal footing. When related to the reality of human suffering, our theology of care must not deny eschatological hope. At the same time, it must actively seek a present, historical response to radical suffering and evil. Without a present and immediate compassionate response, pastoral care, consolation, and hope degenerate into wishful thinking and an excuse to remain indifferent and passive in the face of radical suffering and injustice.

African American women's experience, womanist analysis of hope in the midst of radical suffering, and theodicy influenced by feminist analysis of women's experience point to redemption not in suffering, but in suffering defied. "We will not be overcome; with the help of the Lord Jesus who defeated evil, we will not be overcome. We will see our children and grandchildren live in a world different than ours." This transforming hope is embodied by active, communal defiance of circumstances, people, and systems that corrode the human spirit. Suicidal despair and self-destruction are cut short in the face of defiant hope.

In a much smaller way, mental health studies show that resistance is effective to sustain those who suffer with chronic physical disease, mental illness, addiction, or traumatic stress—all risk factors for suicide. Therapies that name the character of suffering and teach clients and their families how to form a community of resistance show markedly better recovery and survival rates in follow-up than other forms of help.[27] Most successful treatment programs embrace some form of social activism to undermine the physical and social power of a disease. For example, most trauma recovery programs encourage wounded people, as part of their own recovery, to find active ways to join with and protect others from the evil of horrific trauma. Local mental health associations sponsor depression screening days, and survivors of suicide organize to educate the public about suicide prevention.

Active resistance, or defiance, is an important pastoral care position that protects at-risk people from conditions that encourage self-destruction. This can be lived out congregationally through pastoral counseling, discipleship, and preaching and teaching. Pastors can help individuals identify undeserved suffering and connect them to people and communities that are already engaged in active resistance. This might include psycho-education programs at a local hospital for those who suffer from chronic depression. It might also mean establishing a group for a growing number of church members who suffer from episodic or chronic depression.

Discipleship can also be an important location for defiance, especially if it takes place within a context of congregational mentoring. In the context of secure, ongoing relationships, pastoral leaders can help depressed or at-risk-for-suicide individuals find religious resources and a personal spiritual framework for defying the processes and impulses that threaten life.

Preaching and Teaching

Finally, pastoral care can take a more central place in preaching and teaching. The liturgical calendar can draw attention to how human suffering intersects with discipleship and congregational life. This is central to the gospel. Sermons and lessons can use primary biblical themes, such as the Exodus, Babylonian exile, and Jesus' ministry, to highlight God's presence in human history and how collaborative resistance changes the conditions of suffering. Preaching these themes can move a congregation toward actions of care and foster defiance in those who face radical suffering and self-destruction. These sermon themes also provide an opportunity to articulate theologies supporting health. This may include lessons emphasizing collaborative theologies of resistance, highlighting the protective and healing network effect of life together in communion and how important it is for the community of Christ to explore the gospel hope for those who must manage mental illnesses or other life conditions over which they have little perceived or real control.

4

Responding to Completed Suicide

The call came early Saturday evening. "Pastor, I'm with Jane (a church member). She came home from work this afternoon and found her husband dead. He shot himself. EMS and the police have been here. She's not doing well. Can you come?" There are few calls a pastor can receive that are more difficult. Suicide sets in motion a cascade of questions, actions, and consequences that are unique in pastoral ministry. It is categorically different than sudden accidental death or death by violence. It is a choice that forever alters the future for those left behind, thrusting survivors immediately into an emotional vortex that is deeply personal, shame-bearing, religious, and public. Pastors must be prepared to respond to the complicated grieving related to suicide, the unique religious questions the event raises, and the peculiar social dimensions of suicide stigma. Responding to a suicide requires that pastors have some skill in crisis management and understand its long-term effects. Suicide will have a deep congregational impact and will demand theological response. A completed suicide jars pastor, survivors, and congregation into a process of action and reflection* necessary to preserve life and make personal and theological sense of a horrific event.

---

* Refer to liberative praxis and hermeneutical circulation described in chapter 2.

CRISIS MANAGEMENT

Completed suicide presents an active crisis for a victim's family, friends, and community. The immediate task is to respond to family members and to stabilize a potentially volatile situation. Survivors of suicide have suddenly lost a family member. They may also be subject to secondary trauma related to emergency procedures, police investigations, and insensitive professionals with little sympathy for one who has taken his or her own life.

By definition, crisis is a state of emotional distress that exceeds a person's ability to cope using his or her available resources.[1] Without intervention, crisis can result in significant mental disorganization and have serious life consequences. Models of crisis intervention focus on several common goals:

- de-escalate the crisis experience rapidly to prevent further deterioration;
- restore emotional and physical functioning to at least a pre-crisis state;
- promote growth and improved problem solving;
- identify potential danger signs for negative outcomes such as self-destructive behavior, mental or physical illness, or relational collapse.

According to crisis theory, intervention is straightforward. It is concrete support and action. It is oriented to the here and now. It is structured to contain physical and emotional collapse with an eye toward future growth.

Crisis Intervention and Questions of Faith

Crisis theory is important for ministry, but without a theological foundation it is inadequate. Crisis care has deep roots in Judeo-Christian history and Christian ministry. God's response to Adam and Eve in the garden, prophetic responses to personal and national crisis, and Jesus' response to Peter in the garden of Gethsemane are examples of a dominant theme: God cares when human lives are turned upside down. Such events almost always stimulate profound questions of meaning and faith. Pastoral theologian Charles Gerkin observed that crises force people to examine their faith at three distinct levels.[2] First, crisis is a situation that is inescapable and requires a decision. Second, this decision is usually about whether one will live or die in the face of this situation. Third, the situation is "momentous." Questions of ultimate significance are almost always present. The special circumstance of suicide creates an immediate and existential crucible for inescapable questions about ultimate meaning. Any intervention limited to improving coping skills is inadequate. Pastors must attend to fundamental theological questions embedded in survivors' experience. According to Gerkin, "the purpose of crisis ministry has to do not only with the restoration of persons to the ordinary flow of life experience but also with the transformation of life in harmony with God's purposes. Hope and expectation thus become key ingredients in the stance of ministry in crisis, as does the openness to the reality of suffering that crisis experience entails."[3] Ministry in suicide crisis means balancing psychological survival with interpreting faith meanings symbolized by the event.

Interpreting the relationship between Christian faith and suicide is not easy. There is no clear scriptural referent for guidance. One of the first and clearest theological statements about suicide grew from a fourth-century pastoral concern. Augustine, in his pastoral role as bishop, was confronted by the decision of a group of Christian women who ended their own lives rather than become impure through anticipated rape. His response was twofold. First, he removed motivation for martyr suicide—nothing on earth could defile a believer in such a way that God could not heal it. Augustine took a second theological stand. While Scripture does not specifically condemn suicide, neither does it make it lawful. As scriptural authority, he interpreted the commandment

109

"thou shalt not kill" as an implicit biblical injunction against suicide. This interpretation was the guiding theology of suicide until Thomas Aquinas's more systematic treatment of the subject. In his *Summa Theologica* (2-2) Aquinas declared that all living creatures strive to preserve life, so suicide is contrary to natural law. Second, suicide does not affect only the person who dies. It affects the entire community, and therefore undermines human social obligations. Third, suicide is an act of sin. It substantially usurps God's authority to determine when a person will live or die; it is an act of evil to avoid some lesser evil in human suffering. Finally, Aquinas concluded that suicide was the worst (and unforgivable) sin because one could not repent of suicide after the fact. Aquinas's interpretation of suicide and Christian faith has powerfully influenced Christian thinking about suicide. The hopelessness of suicide victims has been immortalized, for example, in Dante's *Inferno* (where suicide victims inhabit the seventh level of hell beneath murderers and the greedy) and by church doctrine forbidding victims of suicide to be buried in cemeteries consecrated by Catholic priests.

Though Protestant theologians have not declared suicide an unforgivable sin or restricted burial, Augustine's and Aquinas's logic were incorporated into the theology of the Reformation. The Westminster Shorter Catechism (1647) closely follows Augustine by stating that "the sixth commandment forbiddeth the taking away of our own life, or the life of our neighbor unjustly, or whatsoever tendeth thereunto." Likewise, Dietrich Bonhoeffer illustrates Aquinas's presence in Protestant conceptions of suicide by asserting that only God has the right to determine the end of life. Only God knows the goal of life, and it is God's will to lead one to it. To end one's own life under any circumstance is to undermine God's will: "Even if a person's earthly life has become a torment for him, he must commit it intact to God's hand, from which it came."[4]

In recent years, the Catholic church has revised its theology of suicide as the unforgivable sin and Protestant theologians have continued to explore nuances of self-direction, sin, and forgiveness in suicide. Nevertheless, this history—and Dante's images—are deeply embedded in the Christian community's collective consciousness. In most suicide events, pastors must attend to this reality as a deliberate part of their crisis response and ongoing care. Christian people will be confronted with the "unpardonable sin" of their loved one's death through their own internalized theology, remnants of Christian history, or others' insensitive and less informed theological pronouncements. Stabilizing a suicide crisis will mean receiving with sensitivity fears about how suicide will affect a loved one's relationship with God and his or her eternal destiny. The psychological needs of crisis de-escalation may require simple reassurance—to paraphrase the apostle Paul (Rom. 8:35, 38-39), what can separate us from the love of Christ? I am convinced that *nothing* in life or death, no power seen or unseen, not anything in the past or future, nothing in all creation can separate one of God's children from the love of God that is in Christ Jesus. At the same time, a sensitive pastor will also recognize that beyond reassurance, an event such as suicide will often forcefully thrust pastor, survivor, and the congregational community into a longer process of interpretation. Hermeneutical circulation can be used over time to integrate new meanings into personal and congregational narratives.

Suicide crisis may raise other central issues of faith that must be addressed as part of de-escalation. Losing a loved one to suicide can threaten images of God that have been the foundation of daily coping. For instance, where was the God who was supposed to watch over loved ones and protect them from harm? A survivor whose belief system insists that all events are under God's immediate control—or that all events take place for the greater glory of God—may find his or her fundamental faith in God shattered. De-escalation will be particularly difficult when individuals lose both a loved one and their own concept of God to suicide. In these circumstances, de-escalation will most likely mean intensive pastoral presence and support, without trying to answer emotionally overpowering questions. Leslie Smith Townsend's four stages of pastoral presence[5] can be helpful. Rather than trying to answer questions that may result in increased destabilization, pastors can embody the presence of Christ by:

- **Listening.** The pastor's task is to create a hospitable space and become a nonjudgmental, caring presence that invites disclosure. Within this safety, active listening can help a pastor hear the fullness of a parishioner's experience. Listening means listening to words and paying attention to contextual factors that express meaning, such as voice tone, eye contact, facial expression, or the context in which words are spoken.
- **Imagining.** This stage takes the words and emotions expressed by the survivor and imagines what it would be like to be in another person's place. In this stage, pastors must set aside the safety of their emotional distance from the suicide and put themselves in the place of their parishioner. Imagine what it is like to lose a loved one to suicide. Imagine what it is like to lose a treasured image of God. Imagine being unable to find the love of God for one's self or the one who has died. This kind of imagination allows full appreciation of experience. It is not restricted by the limitation of language and gives us an emotional, untranslatable, and visceral understanding of a survivor's despair. Many pastors find this kind of experience too uncomfortable and so avoid this stage of connection.
- **Empathizing.** Imagining sets the stage for empathy. Coming close to another's experience through imagining can produce two results: self-absorption on the pastor's part or a sense of shared humanity as the pastor finds common ground with a survivor. Self-absorption short-circuits pastoral response. This happens when a pastor confronts his or her own vulnera-

bilities, and these become the focus rather than the survivor's experience. For instance, imagining loss of a spouse to suicide may spark reliving the loss of a loved one or stimulate fear for one's own deeply loved family members. Absorption in one's own fear or sorrow leaves little room for empathy. Accurate empathy allows us to touch our own human vulnerability at a point of common humanity and enter the world of another's experience. Empathy is the act of emotionally holding hands as we stare together into the same abyss of sorrow and know there are few answers.

- **Connecting.** Pastoral connection is the result of the previous three stages. Words may or may not be spoken. Connection takes place when survivors know they are heard, understood, and accompanied on a horrific journey. Connection is often quiet. It can be expressed simply by physical presence that cries alongside deep grief, a word or two spoken in care for the survivor, and at times a short prayer expressing the experience apprehended through empathy. Connecting usually does not mean offering quick and ill-formed reassurances or effort to change the mind of a survivor about the meaning of a suicide. Pastoral presence that de-escalates crisis is more like running alongside the disciples fleeing in sorrow from the crucifixion or sitting with Mary beneath Jesus' dead body than engaging in meaningful theological talk along the road to Emmaus. That walk must come later.

Crisis Intervention: Debriefing

Pastoral presence also forms a foundation for debriefing. This intervention encourages survivors to repeat their horrific story. Giving language to experience helps a survivor manage shock, establishes the reality of the event, and begins the long-term process of integrating the event and its meanings into the survivor's life story. This process may last hours, days

113

or weeks.* It is likely to be a repetitive process in the hours and days following a suicide. The story of loss expressed in words provides a stabilizing center point for vacillation between denial ("This isn't really happening! I'll wake up from this nightmare soon.") and sudden, overwhelming clarity that strips away all psychological defense against the pain of loss. This process cannot be changed and must not be short-circuited by well-meaning responses meant to reduce the emotional valence of either denial or collapse. Pastoral care embodies God's presence at the depths of human experience. It must be capable of hearing the full story of pain expressed verbally, emotionally, and physically. Debriefing gives survivors permission to reinterpret experience through telling and retelling their story of loss from the dual perspectives of denial and despair. This task requires intensive pastoral presence in the form of extended periods of time and immense psychic energy. Good judgment is also required. A pastor must be present enough to listen well and provide support but also sensitive enough to avoid being intrusive or encouraging unproductive dependency.

Suicide presents special circumstances that call for special care in debriefing. In some cases, religious and personal meanings force denial that a loved one has taken his or her own life. Suicide carries multiple social meanings of personal rejection and failure in tandem with its religious meanings. Beneath this load, survivors may refuse to accept a medical or legal finding of suicide. This denial (sometimes in the face of overwhelming evidence) may range from quiet insistence that authorities are mistaken, to rage at a system that will not see the "truth" about a loved one's death, or to delusional thoughts of a conspiracy to cover up what "really happened" to a loved one. In these circumstances it is the pastor's job to be present in a way that facilitates de-escalation and eventual integration of loss into a survivor's narrative. It is not the

---

*When debriefing conversation is compulsively repeated or increases over a period of weeks, it is important to refer for a psychiatric assessment.

pastor's job to persuade a survivor to accept a suicide pronouncement. Conversations that try to dispel denial or convince a survivor that it is in his or her best interest to accept the reality of a suicide may undermine pastoral presence and hinder later spiritual growth. If intense denial derails crisis management or seriously impedes daily functioning, survivors should be referred to a pastoral counselor or other mental health professional for evaluation.

Some suicide survivors may be badly traumatized by the gruesome discovery of a loved one's broken body. Debriefing may include listening to disturbing details of death, helping a parishioner find words for the unspeakable, and providing information about the kinds of feelings, flashbacks, and physical reactions trauma survivors can expect. Effective pastoral presence in this kind of fresh trauma will "sit with" a parishioner in a nonanxious way that may keep a survivor's psychic ship from crashing into rocks along the shores of sanity. In some cases, a psychiatric referral may be necessary for medication to control the physical and emotional fallout of intense trauma.

Family and close friends of one who has taken his or her own life often experience intense survivor guilt and a sense of failure. Questions like "Why didn't I see this coming?" or "Why didn't I take his depression more seriously?" often become part of crisis escalation. Debriefing can often reassure and de-escalate this cycle of guilt and failure. No one can fully know another's mind or anticipate another's action.

Crisis Intervention: Organizing Resources

Crisis management can also take very concrete and physical forms. It is not unusual for survivors of suicide to also lose their home temporarily. When a death has taken place at home, family members may not be able to return home before investigations are complete or remnants of violent death are removed. Often people feel unable to return to a house where a spouse or child has taken his or her own life.

Pastors can intervene by organizing resources for a temporary safe place to stay. Some suicide cases may be particularly complex and need resources beyond pastoral care. Again, pastors can mobilize the resources of attorneys to protect the interests of survivors, as well as physicians and social workers when necessary. Finally, pastors may help survivors by protecting them from life-changing decisions made impulsively in the wake of a suicide or other intense loss. Often pastors may be the most trusted caregiver during a critical post-loss time. It is not unusual for people to feel that life is forever changed or that life has ended for them. Irrational thinking may propel survivors toward dramatic action such as ending a career or marriage, impulsively making financial decisions, or making decisions about their own health and future. Pastors can help parishioners manage potentially self-destructive decisions by staying close by, encouraging no sudden moves in the wake of intense crisis, and by referring them to reliable advisors.

~~~~

Though de-escalation sounds like a straightforward, linear process, it is important to remember that humans rarely respond as professionally expected. In reality, crisis and de-escalation are cyclical processes with a natural ebb and flow. Charles Gerkin[6] and other theorists suggest that crisis resolution operates through alternating states of consciousness that vacillate between acceptance and denial. From this perspective, pastors can expect that crisis will de-escalate in a ragged, disjointed way rather than a smooth, linear process of recovery. Practically, this means that parishioners may have periods of relative "recovery" punctuated by episodes of intensely painful regression into crisis experience. Survivors need to be encouraged to reserve self-judgment and to give themselves space and time to make sense of a fundamentally senseless experience.

The third and fourth goals of crisis intervention (promoting growth and identifying potential signs for self-destructive behavior, mental or physical illness, or relational collapse) are not necessarily discrete steps taken after the first two goals (de-escalation and restoring emotional and physical functioning) are complete. Instead, these latter goals are embedded within the action of the former. De-escalation and restoration take place with an eye toward how intervention will promote future growth. Pastoral presence and careful attention to theological interpretation, for instance, are crucial in accomplishing this goal. Helping parishioners into the initial stages of liberative praxis during crisis de-escalation also helps set the stage for personal and spiritual growth once crisis has stabilized. Throughout the process of crisis intervention, pastors must be aware of potential psychological problems that may have negative outcomes. Sometimes, no matter how well an intervention is organized, survivors will collapse beneath emotional and psychological weight. Pastors must be ready to respond with appropriate referral or help with the process of hospitalization. Pastors must also realize that suicide survivors are at risk for suicide themselves. Monitoring survivors' despair and suicidal ideation in the months following loss is an important part of the fourth goal of intervention.

For the sake of clarity, I have described crisis intervention as a process with one survivor. In the wake of suicide, this is rarely the case. A number of family members, friends, and church members may tax a pastor's time and emotion to its limits. It is important to organize a system of pastoral response that relies not only on a senior pastor or minister of pastoral care but also other trained staff and lay leaders capable of responding. Crises are a natural part of life. Pastors can prepare for these by training gifted parishioners to respond to pastoral care emergencies. If the congregation has not established this kind of ministry, a pastor can call gifted church leaders together to help respond to a suicide emergency. These lay ministers should be emotionally healthy enough to manage intense anxiety, spiritually mature enough to manage religious questions with careful judgment, and capable of listening, imagining, empathizing, and connecting. They must also be able to maintain absolute confidentiality in conversations with survivors. The team should meet to outline crisis intervention goals (de-escalate crisis, restore emotional and physical functioning, promote growth and problem solving, identify danger signs), field questions about the suicide, and discuss strategies for intervention. In some cases a pastor may feel inadequately trained or uncomfortable organizing a care team. Most communities have qualified hospital chaplains or pastoral counselors who can help lead the team process.

A funeral following suicide often marks the transition from crisis management to follow-up care. Funeral planning consolidates the reality of loss. Managing the details of death pierces denial and raises theological issues anew. These provide a window for further crisis resolution and opportunities for religious reflection. Planning the service takes special care. Family members may be deeply embedded in a struggle with denial and despair. Some may not accept that suicide has occurred. Others will struggle with feelings of betrayal, guilt, and shame. Most will have some anxiety about the effects of a funeral. Suicide becomes very public when a victim's death is described in liturgy, eulogy, and homily. These are interpretive events and become part of the family and community's narrative.

Primary family members must be included in decisions of how a victim's life is honored and the death is portrayed. Supported by the strength of good pastoral connection, simple questions such as, "What would you like me to say about Sharon?" "Are there things you want to be sure I say?" or "Are there things you want to be sure I don't say?" can highlight potential areas of hope, betrayal, or shame. Discussing these questions can help structure a supportive funeral service, avoid unnecessary public shame, and define areas of concern for future care. Homilies and eulogies should respect boundaries set by primary family members. When families cannot agree on how much to reveal about a suicide, pastors must err on behalf of the most vulnerable in the system. A funeral is not the place to challenge denial or insist that public truth telling is healing. At the same time, a funeral service must be contextually coherent enough to offer comfort and hope to those who know they are surviving a suicide.

FOLLOW-UP CARE

Once an immediate suicide crisis is managed, recovery is the focus of ongoing pastoral care. This usually means less intensive intervention over months or years. Survivors must negotiate a cycle of recovery that includes emotional, relational, and spiritual adjustments. Personal and congregational narratives must be rewritten to incorporate a suicide into life's story in a redemptive way. Individual recovery and congregational recovery are linked. A congregation unable to make sense of a suicide or integrate it into its story is rarely able to provide emotional, spiritual, or reflective theological help to individual survivors. Likewise, individuals unable to move beyond denial, despair, guilt, and shame can undermine congregational recovery. Care must be a multilevel, dynamic, dialogical process that maintains conversation with individual survivors and guides normal congregational processes toward community recovery.

Individual and Family Recovery

Those closest to the suicide victim often require direct, intensive help with recovery. Most approaches to pastoral care in loss are organized around Elizabeth Kubler-Ross's[7] five stages of grief—denial and isolation, anger, bargaining, depression, and acceptance. These approaches are useful but fail to address recovery from the trauma often associated with suicide.

Clinicians have developed a number of methods for trauma recovery over the past twenty years. Most are not appropriate for pastoral care in the parish. However, two models are grounded in recovery as a spiritual process and offer a helpful approach for pastoral ministry. Gerkin's[8] crisis model anchors recovery in a theological process of meaning making. Survivors find meaning in their own life and death by vacillating between acceptance and denial of the loss they must survive. Multiple themes of guilt, anger, shame, and painful questions about God all return eventually to a particular center of gravity—how does a survivor's story of loss intersect with his or her understanding of life in relationship with God and with others? How does this event restructure a sense of self and spiritual meaning? How is God's love and the story of Jesus changed for suicide survivors? What, now, is the story of my life? This recursive, theologically grounded cycle of denial and acceptance flows through the emotional and psychological process of trauma recovery.

Suicide survivors can expect to negotiate several tasks of recovery energized by this oscillation between denial and acceptance. Joel Brende, a psychiatrist specializing in trauma, developed a twelve-theme model[9] to understand recovery tasks. His approach was constructed on a familiar twelve-step framework with the aid of chaplains. It has a conscientious spiritual focus and was designed for use in nonclinical contexts. By modifying his model to fit survivors of suicide, pastors can envision recovery moving in a ragged, circular way through the following twelve tasks, or themes.

- **Power versus victimization.** Survivors of suicide must acknowledge that they were powerless to stop a loved one from the act. They also cannot change the consequences of a suicide for themselves or the ones they love. *Spiritual task: Survivors must find a source of power outside of themselves, in God, that can assure meaning in surviving and in recovering from suicide loss.*
- **Seeking meaning in survival.** Being the one left behind in trauma can be a source of intense pain. It is easy to

lose life's purpose in the wake of suicide. Survival alone is not enough. *Spiritual task: Without a clear purpose, life has little meaning. Consequently, survivors must seek a purpose in having survived and learn to keep an open mind to God leading toward a renewed purpose. Survivors must learn to defy those internal and external elements that would dehumanize by withholding meaning in life.*

- **Trust.** Suicide frequently feels like a personal betrayal. It destroys trust in others, self, and God. Survivors of suicide often do not trust their own feelings, perceptions, and behaviors. *Spiritual task: Learning to trust that God cares about a survivor's well-being and acts through friends, pastors, and professionals who wish to help.*

- **Self-inventory.** Recovery requires ongoing self-examination. Survivors must honestly assess both their positive responses to the tragedy of suicide and the "dark sides" of experience, such as unresolved resentment, blame, or hatred. *Spiritual task: As an act of prayer and worship, survivors must evaluate their guiding thoughts, emotions, and behavior. Both positive and negative attributes must be acknowledged before God and a person they trust, with a commitment to embrace the positive and to work to change the negative with God and others' help.*

- **Anger.** Suicide survivors are often angry. Because anger is easy to identify and express, it often covers other more subtle feelings that remain unexpressed. Consequently, anger can become destructive. Recovery means controlling the destructive dimensions of anger and learning to understand other feelings that may be hidden behind anger. *Spiritual task: Survivors must acknowledge rage toward God and those by whom they feel abandoned or betrayed. Survivors must seek God's help and the help of those they trust to control destructive rage and channel anger constructively.*

- **Fear.** Suicide survivors often face enduring fear of further loss, of exposure, and of an unknown future. Recovery means learning to understand the sources and symptoms of fear, accepting fear as normal and reasonable, and controlling the life-limiting and self-destructive elements of fear. *Spiritual task: With the help of God and others they trust, survivors must learn to name fear and defy those life-robbing and dehumanizing impulses that torment the soul and stifle vitality.*
- **Guilt.** Suicide survivors often suffer from destructive guilt about failures in their relationship with a suicide victim or perceived lapses in protecting the one who has died. Survivors may also feel guilty about intense negative feelings about God, the deceased, and the pain the suicide victim has caused in the survivors' lives. *Spiritual task: With the help of God and someone they trust, survivors must reveal their secret guilt and name their need for self-forgiveness. They must learn to rely on God for the strength to resist internal and external powers that withhold the grace necessary to forgive one's self.*
- **Grief.** Suicide survivors often become stuck in a complicated grief process. Shame and complex feelings of guilt and fear motivate isolation. Distance from important friendships and pastoral relationships short-circuits the tears and reconstructive conversation that remembers what was lost and forms a new story of how life will continue with integrity. *Spiritual task: Survivors must turn to God and others they trust to mourn the death of the suicide victim and the parts of themselves that also died. This will require facing painful memories, accepting tears as God's gift of healing, and being thankful that God and the presence of Christian community can heal sorrows.*
- **Suicide versus life.** Suicide survivors often battle depression for long periods of time. They may believe

they would be better off joining the suicide victim. Recovery means facing the consequences of suicide realistically, learning to believe that the people who care for them want them to stay alive, and resisting impulses to plan their own death. Survivors must decide how much of their own life the suicide of a loved one will dominate. *Spiritual task: Survivors must admit suicidal thoughts, plans, and wishes to God and someone they trust. With the help of God, others, and therapy if necessary, they must turn toward a commitment to life and renewed meaning. With the help of God and friends, survivors must face those parts of life suicide daily consumes and work toward a life-giving balance.*

- **Resentment versus forgiveness.** Suicide survivors had no control in their loved one's choice to end life. Frequently, suicide survivors are shackled by resentment (at times bordering on hate) for the victim who turned their life inside out. This may extend to resenting people who have not had to face suicide. Resentment may be deeply buried beneath guilt and fear. Fear of self and other judgment may keep resentment from ever being voiced. *Spiritual task: Survivors must acknowledge feelings of resentment to God and another person they trust. Resentment nurtured is a breeding ground for hate and can damage the spirit of survivors and others around them. Once named, it can be defied, relinquished to forgiveness and appropriate anger, and integrated into a survivor's particular story of redemption.*

- **Finding a purpose.** Suicide can rob survivors of life purpose. Without a meaningful direction, individuals can circulate endlessly through grief, despair, and resentment, sometimes to the point of self-loathing. Survivors must find a renewed purpose in life that integrates suicide loss into a new life story. Many survivors turn toward what Wendy Farley would call defiance by becoming prevention advocates, supporting survivor groups, sharing their stories, etc. *Spiritual task: With the help of God and trusted others, survivors seek to discover who they are and why they are here. In the light of suicide loss, they must seek God's direction for their new life and discover the role surviving suicide will play in that new direction.*

- **Love and relationship.** Brende suggests simply surviving a trauma is not enough. The darkness that follows is too strong and pervades a survivor's soul. Instead, love must lead one away from the shadows. Love requires action. Only love can overcome the rages, resentment, sorrow, and purposelessness that are constant companions of trauma survivors. Love integrates experience and turns it outward in healing and connecting action. *Spiritual task: Survivors must commit themselves to those whose love they have taken for granted, help those who have suffered as they have, and seek God's strength to love those they have not been able to love.*

Negotiating these themes is not a step-by-step process. A survivor will weave his or her way through individual themes (or sets of themes) that are important in a particular time, place, and set of circumstances. Rarely are they "resolved." Rather, they recycle as survivors confront new dimensions of the denial/acceptance process.

While it is not usually a pastor's job to conduct trauma recovery groups or lead treatment, this thematic framework is useful. First, themes provide a context for ongoing assessment of where parishioners are in their recovery process. Which themes are active now? How has a survivor integrated some themes and not others in his or her personal, family, and congregational relationships? Second, these themes provide a structure for pastoral conversations and theological reflection throughout the recovery process. Pastors can help survivors name current issues of recovery and their spiritual tasks. Care can be structured, for instance, around a parishioner's struggle with power and victimization. These kinds of specific conversations deepen trust in pastoral care, participate in resolving the dilemma between denial and acceptance, and help survivors integrate suicide loss into a renewed and redemptive personal narrative.

Children

Children are often overlooked as suicide survivors. Parents and other well-meaning adults may try to protect the young from suicide realities. This can leave death shrouded in mystery and children anxious about their own and others' safety. Children usually know more than adults think. They hear quiet conversations and adult speculations. Without information, children's imaginations fill in the blanks and form conclusions based on incomplete knowledge. Children's crises must be managed and they, too, must negotiate trauma recovery. Unlike adults, children may not be able to express their thoughts, fears, or emotional experiences verbally. Parents and pastors may not know how much information to give a child or to what extent children should be debriefed about a suicidal death.

Pastoral care for children will take several forms. First, pastors can help parents make decisions about what to reveal to children and how to reveal it. This decision must consider the child's developmental capacities and temperament. In most cases, if adults know that a family member or friend has died from suicide, it is counterproductive to try to withhold it from children. At the same time, details about the suicide may be overwhelming and developmentally inappropriate. In most cases, children should be given basic facts with an ear sensitive to their emotional response. For example, a conversation with a seven-year-old:

(Parent) "Megan, Uncle Joe died last night. That's why we're crying and everyone is sad."

125

(Megan) "Does that mean he went to be with Jesus?"

(Parent) "Yes, it does."

(Megan pauses) "How did he die?"

(Parent) "You will probably hear people talking about this. Uncle Joe committed suicide. Do you know what that means?"

(Megan shakes her head no)

(Parent) "It means, as much as we hate it, he killed himself. We're all very sorry about that."

(Megan) "Why did he do that?"

(Parent) "I'm not sure any of us know for sure. We're all very sad. It will take all of us a while to get used to living without Uncle Joe."

(Megan is silent)

(Parent) "I know this is new to you. I know you can't figure it out right now. I know you will probably have some more questions. I want you to ask anything you want about this whenever you need to. I'll do my best to answer your questions."

This kind of conversation should be followed by careful attention to Megan's behavior and affective expression. Young children have not yet developed an emotional language and are highly sensitive to adult affective cues. If adults around them are anxious or depressed, children will respond in kind. Children may be lost in the shuffle as primary caretakers' lives are disrupted by crises. With no language sufficient to their internal experience, children may develop behavioral symptoms. This may take the form of nightmares, bedwetting, clingy dependency, tantrums, or other nonverbal behavior that calls a parent to their side. Pastors can help parents interpret their children's behavior at a time when a crisis undermines basic parenting skills. Pastors can also help parents find developmentally appropriate answers to children's questions about suicide. It may be necessary to help a parent decide when professional help is needed for a child overwhelmed by the fallout of a suicide.

Pastoral presence is important for children. However, some children may have limited contact with the pastor as congregational leader and may be intimidated by pastoral initiative. In these cases, a child's Sunday school teacher, children's program leader, or youth director may become a significant part of the response team. These leaders are often gifted in communicating with children and may be the best prepared people in the congregation to respond in developmentally appropriate ways.

Finally, pastors must attend to children's long-term recovery from suicide trauma. Like adults, children must learn to manage vacillation between denial and acceptance. They will have to negotiate many of the same recovery themes listed above as they grow in the "nurture and admonition of the Lord" (Eph. 6:4 KJV). Pastors and church leaders must remember that suicide trauma will nuance children's normal emotional and spiritual developmental tasks. As children move through developmental stages, they will need opportunities to process what suicide means personally and religiously as they transition from child to older child, adolescent, or young adult.

Community Resources for Survivors

Recovery from suicide is more than an individual process between pastor and survivor. It is communal. Healing includes mobilizing community and congregational resources to extend care during recovery. Survivors can be referred to pastoral counselors or other mental health professionals for needed therapy. Most communities have programs for survivors of suicide or groups that help adult and child survivors manage the long-term process of recovery. The American Association of Suicidology provides a variety of resources for suicide survivors and those who provide care for survivors.[*] Local support groups can be found in on-line directories[†], and a national organization for survivors provides both support

---

[*] http://www.suicidology.org/displaycommon.cfm?an=1&subarticlenbr=48
[†] http://www.afsp.org/survivor/groups.htm

resources and opportunities to help other suicide survivors.* Pastors can also extend care by training gifted lay leaders to engage in pastoral conversations and structuring worship and congregational life to respond to the recovery needs of survivors.

Suicide Survivors and Congregational Life

A completed suicide can reach deeply into congregational life. Suicidologists estimate that suicide will negatively impact at least ten times as many people as an accidental death or sudden death from illness. Unexpected suicide within a congregation introduces a deep, often unspoken, level of anxiety into congregational life. Well-meaning people will not know how to respond to the public-private knowledge that a member has taken his or her own life. Congregational support for survivors and other vulnerable people in the parish may be immobilized when members don't know how to talk to each other about a taboo death. Information about the suicide may be tightly contained. Sometimes this is the family's wish; often it is a form of congregational denial. To admit that the unspeakable has happened to one of us is to acknowledge that it could happen to any of us.

When suicide takes place within a congregation, pastors face a dilemma. They must balance a family's need for privacy with the congregation's need for enough information to manage its own process of denial and acceptance. Suicide hidden from view tends to be an open secret. Living underground, this secret can take on a life of its own and live for years as a toxic element. It can isolate people from each other, fuel damaging rumors, and abort redemptive reflection. When congregations carry on as if this were a "normal" loss, they stunt their own spiritual growth and put vulnerable members of the congregation at risk for anxiety and depression. There is good evidence that suicide in any community increases the

---

* http://www.survivorsofsuicide.com/index.html

risk for "copycat," or suicide contagion, phenomenon. Rates of suicide increase in communities once the suicide barrier is broken.[10]

Following any suicide, it is important for pastors to form long- and short-term plans for how suicide information is managed, how members traumatized by the event will care for each other, and how congregational life and worship will be structured to help integrate the event into the congregation's narrative. This may take many shapes depending on the size of the church, the constellation and style of church leadership, and the kind and quality of interaction within the congregation. When possible, it is important to express care through central (and usually constant) congregational practices of worship, teaching, and fellowship. This normalizes theological reflection, brings a traumatic event to the center of worship, and lowers the risk that family survivors will be marginalized into specialized trauma recovery programs peripheral to congregational life. The following case study provides one example.

Brown family

One Sunday morning in May, Martha Brown knocked on her seventeen-year-old daughter Susan's bedroom door. It was time to prepare for church. Hearing no answer, she went into the room and uncovered Susan. Susan was not breathing and had no heartbeat. Several prescription pill bottles were on the floor. Martha frantically called 911 and began CPR on Susan. Brad, Martha's husband, was at church for an early leadership meeting. Upon arrival, EMS technicians gathered the pill bottles and transported Susan to the nearest emergency room. Martha called Brad and the couple met at the hospital. Susan could not be resuscitated. Her respiratory system had failed at least an hour before she arrived at the emergency room. The emergency room physician explained that Susan had ingested a large amount of alcohol and swallowed a full month's supply of medication that she took for a mild seizure disorder. She asked Martha and Brad what had precipitated her suicide.

129

Pastor Little had arrived within minutes. He stood with Brad and Martha as they heard that Susan was dead and collapsed into shock. Several telephone calls managed the morning service and arranged care for the couple's younger children. Pastor Little sat with the couple in the emergency room as they completed necessary paperwork and tried to manage the overwhelming impact of their daughter's suicide. Few words were spoken. Martha vacillated between uncontrollable tears and "no! this can't be happening!" Brad sat mute and unresponsive, getting up once to vomit. Pastor Little held hands with Martha and cried with her. A hospital chaplain arrived who knew Pastor Little. He offered spiritual support and any help he could give to facilitate hospital procedures. After a short consultation with Pastor Little, the chaplain prayed with the couple and then sat attentively in a chair close by. After some time, the emergency room physician returned briefly to say that an autopsy would be required before Susan's body could be released. The couple needed to make arrangements with a mortuary to pick up Susan's body and begin the funeral process. Chaplain Perry explained hospital procedures in more detail and provided his contact information for follow-up.

Pastor Little and the couple left the consultation room and found several church members waiting to provide transportation home. For the rest of the day, Pastor Little and a gifted lay leader sat with the Browns and their two younger children. By listening, imagining, empathizing, and connecting he was able to hear the range and depth of their pain. He minimized crisis escalation by listening carefully to Martha tell and retell her story of finding Susan and to Brad blaming himself for not anticipating Susan's suicide. He sat with the couple as they cycled through utter despair and denial. Pastor Little carefully watched the younger children as they alternated between crying, clinging desperately to their parents, and moving away to watch television. He spoke few words in the first hours. Later, Martha spoke her fear that her daughter's suicide put her outside of God's care. Pastor Little was able to talk with the couple and their children about God's unconditional love and the scriptural promise that nothing could separate Susan from the love of God.

Information about Susan's death would spread quickly, so Pastor Little made time to arrange a congregational intervention. He briefly consulted with Martha and Brad, asking their permission to talk with church members about this tragedy. They agreed the congregation should know both that Susan had died and that she had taken her own life. However, they also agreed that Pastor Little should discourage speculation about Susan's motivation. He would reinforce the fact that much was still unknown about her death. Pastor Little next contacted a pastoral counselor and the chaplain from the emergency room. He asked them to consult with each other and to be available for a crisis debriefing at the church early that evening. Both agreed. Church leaders used a congregational calling tree to notify members that emergency meetings would be held at the church to share information about Susan's death. Callers gave priority to notifying youth and their parents.

Later that day, prior to the meeting, Pastor Little discussed intervention goals with the pastoral counselor and chaplain. All agreed that information about Susan's death was widespread. Several teens had seen Susan the night she died. They knew she had suffered a painful breakup in previous days and was discouraged about her seizure disorder. She drank Saturday night and had gone home despondent. The team acknowledged that the church's youth would be at increased risk for trauma symptoms and suicide contagion. Parents would be at risk for increased anxiety about their children and would experience vicarious trauma through the Browns' loss. Younger children would witness adult and youth grief and would have grief of their own. Many might be incapacitated by adult anxiety and would be unable to ask important questions. Together, the crisis team decided to meet separately with adults, youth, and children. They defined several tasks:

1. *To state basic facts.* The Browns and the church had suffered a tragic loss. Susan had died. Martha had

found her in bed not breathing. She could not be revived at the hospital. According to physicians, Susan had taken her own life.

2. *To define the purpose of intervening with the congregation.* The meeting was meant to help congregation members through the initial stages of a shared crisis. It was to be a time for mutual support grounded in a shared history of worship and spiritual life.

3. *To debrief the crisis.* Church members would be given accurate information about Susan's death and the Browns' well-being. The team would answer any questions they could and listen to church members' stories and feelings about Susan's life and death. Participants would be encouraged to tell their own stories of what they had heard, what they knew, what they feared, and how this event was affecting them.

4. *To inform participants about the nature of crisis, trauma, and recovery.* The team would outline some common trauma-related experiences church members might encounter in the days and weeks after Susan's death. Many would feel shock, numbness, outrage, or fear. Some would try to block out the experience altogether. Most would feel confused and sometimes anxious about their own lives or loved ones. Children and youth might have trouble sleeping, awaken with disturbing dreams, develop unexplained fears about everyday life, or have emotional reactions that do not fit circumstances. Adults might experience an increase in generalized anxiety, hypervigilance with their own teens, or a sudden increase in general anxiety. It would not be uncommon for survivors of any age to have depressive feelings or intrusive images of Susan's death. They would be instructed to call one of the team if these symptoms were unmanageable.

5. *To respond to religious and theological myths or concerns.* The team would carefully listen for reli-

gious misunderstandings about suicide that would complicate crisis de-escalation or trauma recovery. They would not correct problematic statements during the meeting unless they held genuine potential for damage. Instead, they would construct a list of theological themes that would need later interpretation. During the meeting, the team would emphasize the scriptural message of God's care in crisis and God's persistent love for Susan and her family.

6. *To give people information about where to get further help if needed.* The team would distribute a sheet with Pastor Little's telephone number and several lay leaders capable of listening and facilitating a referral. Participants would be instructed to call if they needed to talk further about Susan's death or troubling symptoms related to trauma.

After meeting with congregational groups, the team met to discuss their experience and to identify people needing follow-up. They agreed to stay in close contact in the following month to assess if further congregational meetings were necessary.

In the two days following Susan's death, Pastor Little worked with the Browns to structure a funeral that balanced tragic loss with hope. The liturgy and homily did not highlight Susan's suicide, but neither did it ignore the fact that Susan took her own life. Within the message of hope and loss, the Browns arranged a eulogy that expressed their wish that Susan's death would have meaning—perhaps by knowing Susan took her own life, another teen might make a different choice.

In the months following Susan's funeral, Pastor Little kept in careful contact with Susan and Brad. He referred them to a Survivors of Suicide group and to family counseling with a pastoral counselor. In addition, Pastor Little continued to meet with the couple weekly. These sessions helped keep track of the family's progress through the twelve themes of trauma recovery and provided an opportunity to name religious and theological problems emerging from their experience. Pastor

Little also paid close attention to congregational processes. He understood that congregational trauma required corporate theological reflection and a revision of the community's story. Susan's suicide was a jarring event that must stimulate hermeneutical circulation to answer important questions. These might include: How does a congregation make sense of such an oppressive event? How does this suicide articulate previously unseen forms of oppression that resulted in hopelessness and death? What does the gospel message have to say about such hopelessness? What does it say about congregational adjustments needed to resolve a trauma and make meaning from suicide loss? How does suicide impact a congregation's guiding theology? How does Susan's death expand our understanding of God and the gospel of Christ? What does Susan's death mean for a congregation's future, for its youth's future?

In the week after Susan's death, Pastor Little met with the church's ministry team. He began the cycle of liberative praxis by naming Susan's death as a "jarring experience" that started congregational hermeneutical circulation (review chapter 2, fig. 2). The group discussed how they themselves struggled to make sense of a teen suicide. Susan was a well-liked teen and had been active in the youth group. Several parents, concerned about suicide contagion, had asked what the church would do to help youth recover and protect them from increased suicide risk. The ministry team recognized they were already at step two of hermeneutical circularity. They found their community's faith resources inadequate for this situation. Turning to theological sources with new questions (step three) would take several forms and require several action-reflection steps over the following three months. First, Pastor Little would review Scripture and theological literature about suicide. He would also consult with his pastoral counseling and chaplain colleagues to deepen his information about grief and trauma from pastoral theological and behavioral sciences sources. Using this information, Pastor Little would focus his preaching on important questions about life, death, suicide, and recovery. His plan was not to preach "solutions," but invite the congregation into the cycle of action-reflection beginning with four basic questions: "How can we understand what has happened?" "How does what has happened impact our understanding of God's love?" "How do we care for each other in such tragedy?" "How do we recover from this tragedy?"

In addition to a revised preaching agenda, Pastor Little also scheduled a conversation group on Sunday evenings. Leadership of this group would be shared among the ministry team. This group would encourage discussion of the congregation's experience, provide time to wrestle with theological dilemmas, and help the congregation monitor its own progress through trauma recovery. The discussion would begin each week with (1) an important topic from Pastor Little's sermon, (2) a relevant scripture text for group interpretation, or (3) reflection on an emotional experience in the congregation related to the twelve themes of recovery or the denial/acceptance process. The group would also be the place where concrete actions of care could be formed and brought back for reflection (steps three and four of hermeneutical circularity). The ministry team would listen carefully to parishioners in other contexts to help guide topic selection and revise the action-reflection process as necessary. Pastor Little would also stay in close contact with the Browns. He would assure the continuity of their individual care and make sure congregational responses did not overstep important boundaries of privacy or diminish the family's central place in the community's experience.

The youth of the church were a special concern. They needed to be included in the reflective process but were unlikely to attend a Sunday evening group. The ministry team agreed to invite a pastoral counselor with training in trauma debriefing to lead the youth Sunday school program for two weeks. This would encourage conversation and model listening to adolescent grief to adult teachers. Another purpose for this intervention was to set reflective conversations in motion. This would help youth leaders form a structure for steps three and four of hermeneutical circularity. For the next three months, youth Sunday school classes (like the adult discussion group on Sunday night), would interact around central questions raised by sermons, experience, or biblical text. Either youth leaders or designated representatives would take new theological insights to the Sunday evening group. Children's Sunday school teachers would listen for themes of loss and fear or questions about suicide in their interactions with children. These themes would be addressed in classes as they arose and taken to the reflection group.

Over a period of three months the ministry team was able to monitor individual church member's progress through themes of recovery and cycles of denial and acceptance. Working together reflectively, the congregation integrated a deeper theology of mutual care and expanded its understanding of God's presence in traumatic loss (step five, hermeneutical circularity). They learned to talk with each other about deeply existential experience and found ways to interpret the gospel in the light of incomprehensible loss.

Response and Reflection

This example provides one model for how a pastor and congregation can respond to a completed suicide. In truth, congregations are usually much more complex and less cooperative than a single case study can capture. Rarely does a pastor have the luxury of managing one crisis at a time; the best plans can be derailed by the everyday messiness of congregational life. At the same time, intentional response and reflection (tempered by creativity and flexibility) are necessary to guide congregational recovery. Finally, suicide recovery is an ongoing, recycling process. Pastors must be aware that survivors and congregations will relive trauma on anniversaries of a suicide, weddings, funerals, graduations, and birth of new children. It is not unlikely that suicide survivors will need specific, suicide-related pastoral care in each major life transition through a full generation of the family life cycle.

Conclusion

Writing this book meant talking with pastors about suicide in the parish. To a person those consulted agreed: nothing in seminary or continuing education prepared them to respond when they had to face suicide in the congregation. Two themes were evident in these conversations. First, it is frightening to respond to a suicidally depressed church member. Pastors are uncertain about what responsibility they have for someone who is actively thinking of ending their own life. Overreacting, by calling in authorities prematurely for example, can result in chaos and congregational disruption. People shamed by pastoral overreaction can feel betrayed and choose isolation over congregational connection. Failing to take depression seriously can result in death. This is a frightening dilemma. Psychological referral helps, but it does not take the person out of the congregation or relieve the pressure on those who live with the person.

Second, pastors feel helpless when called to the bedside of someone who has tried to take his or her own life or to the side of a family whose loved one has succeeded in suicide. How do Christians speak of suicide? How does a pastor speak directly about suicide with someone who has made an attempt without shaming, moralizing, or promising false hope? How does a pastor manage historic Christian doctrines about suicide when comforting a family whose loved one has just taken his or her own life? How does a congregation talk about a suicide of one of their members? Responding to suicide in any of its forms is not easy.

In this text I addressed both practical and theological concerns for pastors along the suicide continuum. I have not tried to construct a theology of suicide or a standard manual for pastoral response. Suicide is too varied for either. My intent in this book is to help pastors understand what *this* suicide (thought, attempt, or death) means within *this* congregation at *this* time with *these* people. My hope is that this text provides interpretive resources and a reflective strategy that can help transform suicide into redemptive meaning within congregations and the families of those who survive.

Notes

INTRODUCTION

1. Albert Camus, *The Myth of Sisyphus and Other Essays*, trans. Justin O'Brien (New York: Random House, 1955).

2. Anton J. L. van Hooff, "A Historical Perspective on Suicide," in *Comprehensive Textbook of Suicidology*, ed. R. W. Maris, A. L. Berman, and M. M. Silverman (New York: Guilford Press, 2000).

3. Plato, *Laws* IX found in *The Collected Dialogues of Plato*, ed. Edith Hamilton and Huntington Cairns (Princeton, N.J.: Princeton University Press, 1989), 1432.

4. S. L. Denker, "Suicide in the Hebrew Bible and the Rabbinic Tradition," in *Clergy Response to Suicidal Persons and Their Family Members*, ed. D. C. Clark (Chicago: Exploration Press, 1993).

5. Ibid.

6. R. W. Maris, "Ethical, Religious, and Philosophical Issues in Suicide," in *Comprehensive Textbook of Suicidology*, ed. R. W. Maris, A. L. Berman, and M. M. Silverman (New York: Guilford Press, 2000).

7. J. R. Willis, *A History of Christian Thought: From Apostolic Times to St. Augustine* (Hicksville, N.Y.: Exposition Press, 1976).

8. Ibid., 69.

9. H. Anderson, "A Protestant Perspective on Suicide," in *Clergy Response to Suicidal Persons and Their Family Members*, ed. D. C. Clark (Chicago: Exploration Press, 1993).

10. United Methodist Church, *Book of Resolutions* (Nashville: United Methodist Publishing House, 2004).

CHAPTER 1. ASSESSING SUICIDE POTENTIAL IN THE PARISH

1. M. M. Lineham and J. A. Laffaw, "Suicidal Behaviors among Clients of an Outpatient Clinic Versus the General Population," *Suicide and Life-Threatening Behavior* 12 (1982).

2. C. R. Pfeffer, R. Plutchik, and M.S. Mizruchi, "Suicidal Behavior in Child Psychiatric Inpatients and Outpatients and in Non-Patients," *American Journal of Psychiatry* 143 (1986).

3. Hamilton Depression Scale http://healthnet.umassmed.edu/mhealth/ HAMD.pdf. A variety of depression screening tools can be found at http://www.medalreg.com (users must register free of charge and use links to depression evaluation).

4. World Health Organization, "Mastering Depression in Primary Care," (2005). http://www.pdptoolkit.co.uk/Files/wellclosetraining/wellclosecon sult/training/DEPRESSION/mastering_depression_in_primary.htm#2

5. R. W. Maris, "Introduction to the Study of Suicide," in *Comprehensive Textbook of Suicidology*, ed. R. W. Maris, A. L. Berman, and M. M. Silverman (New York: Guilford Press, 2000), R. W. Maris, "Suicide, Gender, and Sexuality," in *Comprehensive Textbook of Suicidology*, ed. R. W. Maris, A. L. Berman, and M. M. Silverman (New York: Guilford Press, 2000).

6. National Center for Health Statistics, (2004).

7. J. Merril et al., "Alcohol and Attempted Suicide," *British Journal of Psychiatry* 87 (1992).

8. A. T. Beck and R. A. Steer, "Clinical Predictors of Eventual Suicide," *Journal of Affective Disorders* 17 (1989).

9. G. E. Murphy and R. D. Wentzel, "The Lifetime Risk of Suicide in Alcoholism," *Archives of General Psychiatry* 47 (1990).

10. J. R. Rogers, "Suicide and Alcohol," *Journal of Counseling and Development* 70 (1992).

11. B. L. Tanney, "Psychiatric Diagnoses and Suicidal Acts," in *Comprehensive Textbook of Suicidology*, ed. R. W. Maris, A. L. Berman, and M. M. Silverman (New York: Guilford Press, 2000).

CHAPTER 2. SUICIDE ATTEMPTS, CARE, AND RECOVERY

1. R. W. Maris, "Suicide Attempts and Methods," in *Comprehensive Textbook of Suicidology*, ed. R. W. Maris, A. L. Berman, and M. M. Silverman (New York: Guilford Press, 2000).

2. P. W. O'Carroll et al., "Beyond the Tower of Babel: A Nomenclature for Suicidology," *Suicide and Life-Threatening Behavior* 26 (1996).

3. K. Hawton et al., "Motivational Aspects of Deliberate Self-Poisoning in Adolescence," *British Journal of Psychiatry* 141 (1982).

4. In *Pastoral Care with Stepfamilies: Mapping the Wilderness* (St. Louis: Chalice Press, 2000), I have suggested that families stressed by non-normative events (such as divorce, gay or lesbian children, etc.) lose a share of the cultural narrative that defines a "good" family. Help often comes in the form of advice on how better to approximate "normal." Those who can manage this by subjugating important parts of their story find some measure of reconciliation and grace. Those who cannot are marginalized. This dynamic is particularly active for people and families surviving a suicide attempt.

5. Robert McAfee Brown, *Theology in a New Key: Responding to Liberation Themes* (Philadelphia: Westminster Press, 1978).

6. For a more complete description of this method see: L. L. Townsend, *Pastoral Care with Stepfamilies: Mapping the Wilderness* (St. Louis, Mo.: Chalice Press, 2000).

7. B. Gill-Austern, "Love Understood as Self-Sacrifice and Self-Denial: What Does It Do to Women?" in *Through the Eyes of Women: Insights for Pastoral Care*, ed. J. S. Moessner (Minneapolis: Fortress Press, 1996).

8. B. Miller-McLemore, "Family and Work: Can Anyone Have It All?" in *Religion, Feminism, and the Family*, ed. A. Carr and M. S. Van Leeuwen (Louisville, Ky.: Westminster John Knox Press, 1996), 291.

9. R. W. Maris, "The Relation of Nonfatal Suicide Attempts to Completed Suicides," in *The Assessment and Prediction of Suicide*, ed. R. W. Maris et al. (New York: Guilford Press, 1992).

10. R. W. Maris, A. L. Berman, and M. M. Silverman, *Comprehensive Textbook of Suicidology* (New York: Guilford Press, 2000).

11. J. M. Toolan, "Suicide in Children and Adolescents," *American Journal of Psychotherapy* 29 (1975).

12. M. A. Schuckit, and J. J. Schuckit "Substance Use and Abuse: A Risk Factor in Youth Suicide," in *Alcohol, Drug Abuse, and Mental Health Administration Report of the Secretary's Task Force on Youth Suicide*. Vol. 2: Risk Factors for Youth Suicide (DHHS Publication no. ADM 89-1622). Washington, D.C.: U.S. Government Printing Office, 1989.

13. Hawton et al., "Motivational Aspects of Deliberate Self-Poisoning in Adolescence."

14. J. Bancroft et al., "The Reasons People Give for Taking Overdoses: A Further Inquiry," *British Journal of Psychiatry* 52 (1979).

15. A. G. Kaplan and R. B. Klein, "Women and Suicide," in *Suicide: Understanding and Responding*, ed. D. J. Jacobs (Madison, Conn.: International Universities Press, 1989).

16. R. W. Maris, "Suicide, Gender, and Sexuality," in *Comprehensive Textbook of Suicidology*, ed. R. W. Maris, A. L. Berman, and M. M. Silverman (New York: Guilford Press, 2000).

17. E. Cummings and C. Lazar, "Kinship Structure and Suicide: A Theoretical Link," *Canadian Review of Sociology and Anthropology* 18 (1981).

18. C. C. Neuger, "Women's Depression: Lives at Risk," in *Women in Travail and Transition*, ed. M. Glaz and Stephenson-Moessner (Minneapolis: Fortress Press, 1991).

19. C. C. Neuger, "Narratives of Harm," in *In Her Own Time*, ed. Stephenson-Moessner (Minneapolis: Fortress Press, 2000).

20. P. Cooper-White, "Opening the Eyes," in *In Her Own Time*, ed. Stephenson-Moessner (Minneapolis: Fortress Press, 2000).

21. K. Shaunesey et al., "Suicidality in Hospitalized Adolescents: Relationship to Prior Abuse," *American Journal of Orthopsychiatry* 63 (1993).

22. Neuger, "Women's Depression: Lives at Risk."

23. T. F. Dugan and M. L. Belfer, "Suicide in Children: Diagnosis, Management, and Treatment," in *Suicide: Understanding and Responding*, ed.

D. J. Jacobs and H. N. Brown (Madison, Wis.: International Universities Press, 1989).

24. M. Kovacs, D. Goldston, and D. Gatsonis, "Suicidal Behaviors and Childhood-Onset Depressive Disorders: A Longitudinal Investigation," *Journal of the American Academy of Child Psychiatry* 32 (1993).

25. R. W. Maris et al., *The Clinical Prediction of Suicide* (New York: Guilford Press, 1992).

26. S. G. Schneider, N. L. Farberow, and G. N. Kruks, "Suicidal Behavior in Adolescent and Adult Gay Men," *Suicide and Life-Threatening Behavior* 19 (1989). A. H. Faulkner and K. Cranston, "Correlates of Same-Sex Behavior in a Random Sample of Massachusetts High School Students," *American Journal of Public Health* 8 (1998).

27. G. Ramifedi et al., "The Relationship between Suicide Risk and Sexual Orientation: Results of a Population-Based Study," *Pediatrics* 87 (1991).

28. Maris et al., *The Clinical Prediction of Suicide.*

29. R. W. Maris and P. A. Nisbet, "Age and the Lifespan," in *Comprehensive Textbook of Suicidology*, ed. R. W. Maris, A. L. Berman, and M. M. Silverman (New York: Guilford Press, 2000).

30. R. W. Maris, *Pathways to Suicide: A Survey of Self-Destructive Behaviors* (Baltimore: Johns Hopkins University Press, 1981).

CHAPTER 3. SUICIDE VULNERABILITY AND LIFE IN CHRISTIAN COMMUNITY

1. A few well-known studies demonstrate that prayer and meditation have positive effects for treatment of both physical and psychological disorders. See, for instance: V. B. Carson, "Prayer, Meditation, Exercise, Special Diets: Behaviors of the Hardy Person with HIV/AIDS," *Journal of the Association of Nurses in AIDS Care*, 4 (1993): 18-28; K. H. Kaplan, D. L. Goldenberg, and M. Galvin-Nadeu, "The Impact of Meditation-based Stress Reduction Program on Fibromyalgia," *General Hospital Psychiatry*, 15 (1993): 284-89.

2. A. B. Newberg and E. G. D'Aquili, "The Neuropsychology of Spiritual Experience," in *Handbook of Religion and Mental Health*, ed. H. Koenig (New York: Academic Press, 1998), 75-94.

3. Émile Durkheim, *Le Suicide: Etude de Sociologie* (Paris: Alcan, 1897).

4. G. W. Allport, *The Individual and His Religion* (New York: Macmillan, 1960).

5. V. Genia and D. Shaw, "Religion, Intrinsic-Extrinsic Orientation, and Depression," *Review of Religious Research* 32, no. 3 (1991); P. J. Watson et al., "Sin, Depression, and Narcissism," *Review of Religious Research* 29 (1988); P. J. Watson, R. J. Morris, and R. W. Hood, "Sin and Self-Functioning, Part 4: Depression, Assertiveness, and Religious Commitments," *Journal of Psychology and Theology* 17 (1989).

6. W. L. Ventis, "The Relationship between Religion and Mental Health," *Journal of Social Issues* 51 (1995).

7. C. H. Hackney and G. S. Sanders, "Religiosity and Mental Health: A Meta-Analysis of Recent Studies," *Journal for the Scientific Study of Religion* 42 (2003); J. M. Salsman and C. R. Carlson, "Religious Orientation, Mature Faith, and Pychological Distress: Elements of Positive and Negative Associations," *Journal for the Scientific Study of Religion* 44, no. 2 (2005).

8. H. G. Koenig, ed., *Handbook of Religion and Mental Health* (New York: Academic Press, 1998).

9. Hackney and Sanders, "Religiosity and Mental Health: A Meta-Analysis of Recent Studies."

10. D. M. Anglin, O. S. Kamieka, and N. J. Kaslow, "Suicide Acceptability and Religious Well-Being: A Comparative Analysis in African American Suicide Attempters and Non-Attempters," *Journal of Psychology and Theology* 33, no. 2 (2005); L. A. Cooper et al., "How Important Is Intrinsic Spirituality in Depression Care?" *Journal of General Internal Medicine* 16 (2001); K. E. Early, *Religion and Suicide in the African-American Community* (Westport, Conn.: Greenwood Publishing Group, 1992); K. E. Early and R. L. Akers, " 'It's a White Thing': An Exploration of Beliefs About Suicide in the African American Community," *Deviant Behavior* 14 (1993).

11. K. E. Early and R. L. Akers, " 'It's a White Thing': An Exploration of Beliefs About Suicide in the African American Community," *Deviant Behavior* 14 (1993).

12. L. A. Cooper et al., "How Important Is Intrinsic Spirituality in Depression Care?" *Journal of General Internal Medicine* 16 (2001).

13. Anglin, Kamieka, and Kaslow, "Suicide Acceptability and Religious Well-Being: A Comparative Analysis in African American Suicide Attempters and Non-Attempters."

14. K. I. Pergament and C. R. Brant, "Religion and Coping," in *Handbook of Religion and Mental Health,* ed. H. G. Koenig (New York: Academic Press, 1998).

15. W. E. Oates, *When Religion Gets Sick* (Philadelphia: Westminster Press, 1970).

16. Ibid.

17. E. P. Wimberly, *Relational Refugees: Alienation and Reincorporation in African American Churches and Communities* (Nashville: Abingdon, 2000).

18. Ibid., 32.

19. E. B. Crawford, *Hope in the Holler: A Womanist Theology* (Louisville: Westminster John Knox Press, 2002).

20. Ibid., xi.

21. Ibid., 117.

22. Ibid., xii.

23. Ibid., 114.

24. W. Farley, *Tragic Vision and Divine Compassion: A Contemporary Theodicy* (Louisville, Ky.: Westminster/John Knox Press, 1990).

25. Ibid., 58.

26. Ibid., 114.

27. W. R. Shadish and S. A. Baldwin, "Meta-Analysis of MFT Interventions," in *Effectiveness Research in Marriage and Family Therapy*, ed. D. H. Sprenckle (Alexandria, Va.: AAMFT, 2002).

CHAPTER 4. RESPONDING TO COMPLETED SUICIDE

1. L. A. Hoff, *People in Crisis: Understanding and Helping*, 4th ed. (San Francisco: Wiley Trade Publishing, 1995).

2. C. V. Gerkin, "Crisis Ministry," in *Dictionary of Pastoral Care and Counseling, Expanded Edition*, ed. R. Hunter (Nashville: Abingdon Press, 2005).

3. Ibid., 248.

4. Dietrich Bonhoeffer, *Ethics* (New York: Macmillan, 1955).

5. L. S. Townsend, "Four Stages of Pastoral Presence" (Hospice of Louisville, 2004).

6. C. V. Gerkin, *Crisis Experience in Modern Life: Theory and Theology for Modern Life* (Nashville: Abingdon Press, 1979).

7. E. Kubler-Ross, *On Death and Dying* (New York: Touchstone Books, 1969). David Switzer, in *The Dynamics of Grief* (Nashville: Abingdon Press, 1970), proposed a six-stage grieving process that included shock, numbing, struggle between fantasy and reality, breakthrough of grief, selective memory and pain, and acceptance of loss and affirmation of life.

8. Gerkin, *Crisis Experience in Modern Life: Theory and Theology for Modern Life*.

9. J. O. Brende, *Assessment of Post-Traumatic Stress Symptoms: A Twelve-Step Approach* (Columbus, Ga.: Trauma Recovery Publications, 1991), J. O. Brende, *Trauma Recovery for Victims and Survivors: A Twelve-Step Recovery Program for Group Leaders* (Columbus, Ga.: Trauma Recovery Publications, 1994).

10. R. W. Maris, "The Social Relations of Suicides," in *Comprehensive Textbook of Suicidology*, ed. R. W. Maris, A. L. Berman, and M. M. Silverman (New York: The Guilford Press, 2000).